Acquisition Behavior of U.S. Manufacturing Firms, 1946-1965

H. Igor Ansoff
Richard G. Brandenburg
Fred E. Portner
Raymond Radosevich

1971
VANDERBILT UNIVERSITY PRESS
Nashville

Published in 1971
by Vanderbilt University Press
Nashville, Tennessee, U.S.A.

To be published in Great Britain
in 1972
by Associated Business Programmes Limited
17 Buckingham Gate, London S.W. 1, England,
with the title
Twenty Years of Acquisition Behavior in America: A Comparative Study of Mergers and Acquisitions of U.S. Manufacturing Firms, 1946-1965.

An article, entitled "Does Planning Pay? Effects of Planning on Success of Acquisitions in American Firms," based on some of the material dealt with in this study, was published in *Journal of Long-Range Planning,* 3, No. 2 (December 1970), copyright © 1970 by the Pergamon Press of Oxford, England.

International Standard Book Number 0-8265-1174-0
Library of Congress Catalogue Card Number 79-163771

Printed in the United States of America

Composed by Computer Composition, Inc., Nashville, Tennessee
Printed by Western Publishing Company, Inc., Hannibal, Missouri
Bound by Vail-Ballou Press, Inc., Binghampton, New York

THE AUTHORS

H. IGOR ANSOFF   Dean, Graduate School of Management,
                                Vanderbilt University

RICHARD G. BRANDENBURG   Dean, School of Management,
                                State University of New York at Buffalo

FRED E. PORTNER   Research Information Center,
                                Bankers Trust Company, New York

RAYMOND RADOSEVICH   Associate Professor of Management,
                                Graduate School of Management,
                                Vanderbilt University

195984

CONTENTS

LIST OF ILLUSTRATIONS

LIST OF TABLES

PREFACE

The study was performed under a grant from the McKinsey Foundation for Management Research, Incorporated, of New York, which had the patience to give us complete freedom to pursue our work over a period of two years unhampered by demands of progress reporting. The several authors take this opportunity to express our sincere thanks to the Foundation and, in particular, to Warren Cannon, for sympathetic forbearance. The study was initiated at Carnegie-Mellon University; portions were completed at other institutions including the University of Kansas, the State University of New York at Buffalo, and Vanderbilt University.

In the formative stage of our study, we benefited from the assistance of Professor Sam Reid, University of Illinois, Chicago Circle. In the later states, the constructive criticism of two other readers provided us with insights which significantly improved the presentation of the study's results. Assistance was provided at several stages by graduate assistants Jay Avner and Hal Hertenstein; we wish to acknowledge their contribution.

Some of the results of the study, primarily those reported in Chapter 5, were previously published by the present authors and Jay Avner in an article, "Does Planning Pay? The Effect of Planning on Success of Acquisitions in American Firms," *Long Range Planning,* 3, No. 2 (December 1970) 2-7. The authors appreciate the permission granted by the Pergamon Press, Headington Hill Hall, Oxford, for use of this material in the book.

Our particular gratitude goes to executives in a large number of American business firms which have taken the trouble to reply to our lengthy questionnaire and to those firms and individuals who have taken the trouble to explain to us those circumstances which prevented them from responding.

We would also like to express our appreciation to the staff of Vanderbilt University Press, particularly Martha Strayhorn for a splendid editorial effort on a very rough manuscript and Gary Gore, whose production capabilities were invaluable in reproducing the many tables, figures, and programs.

ACQUISITION BEHAVIOR

OF U.S. MANUFACTURING FIRMS, 1946-1965

CHAPTER 1

OVERVIEW OF THE STUDY

Effectiveness of corporate mergers and acquisitions as a means of business growth has long been a subject of considerable interest to both the business and the governmental communities. In recent years this interest has been enhanced by several developments. One is the apparent growth in concentration of economic assets, as described, for example, by analyses of *Fortune*'s 500 largest corporations. Another has been the conglomerate acquisition movement which placed major reliance on mergers as an instrument of growth. A third has been a progressive narrowing of the permissible range of acquisition activities by governmental enforcement agencies and the Supreme Court.

A number of studies have appeared which sought to determine whether mergers and acquisitions were a successful method of growth. Several of these studies are described in Chapter 2, where their relationships to this study are more readily apparent. Some of these works analyzed the financial performance of the acquiring firms and compared them to the total economy; others sought to determine subjective perceptions of successes and failures through questionnaires addressed to the acquiring firms.

This study was prompted by a feeling on the part of the authors that previous analyses were neither comprehensive enough to give a complete assessment of the successes, nor deep enough to relate instances of success to the acquisition behavior of typical firms.

STRUCTURE OF THE STUDY

The study spanned a period of some twenty years in the history of acquisition activity by U.S. manufacturing firms. It consists of three major substudies. The first, based on an extensive questionnaire answered by business firms, sought to analyze the characteristics of acquisition behavior, the degree and type of planning, methods used for discovery and analysis of acquisition alternatives, characteristics of the negotiation, and the methods of post-acquisition integration. We sought to correlate all these modes of

3

behavior to results and, in particular, to the attainment of acquisition objectives as perceived subjectively by management.

The second part of the study was based entirely on *objective* data. Using Compustat data provided by Standard and Poor, we analyzed the financial performance of the acquiring firms during the period 1946-1965. In formulating this analysis, we sought to compare pre- and post-acquisition performance, as well as performance of acquirers and nonacquirers. We also sought to determine whether certain pre-acquisition characteristics, such as growth rate or size, resulted in significantly different acquisition performance.

Third, we correlated typical patterns of acquisition behavior of Part 1 to the financial results of Part 2 to determine whether particular types of behavior are more likely to produce success.

The respective parts of the study are discussed in detail in Chapters 3, 4, and 5. As the study progressed, we found increasingly that our attention was focused on two central questions: (1) Are mergers and acquisitions a more promising growth method than internal expansion? (2) Does deliberate and careful planning of merger activity produce results more successful than unplanned opportunistic behavior? A reader who is not prepared to read the rest of this study may be satisfied with simple answers: "No" to question one and "Yes" to question two. The answer to the second question is, to our knowledge, the first rigorous, quantitative proof that formal planning pays off.

A more patient reader will want to peruse the rest of this chapter for a more extended summary of the results. An involved practitioner of mergers and acquisitions will find a detailed exposition in the remaining chapters.

HOW DO FIRMS CONDUCT MERGERS?–THE QUESTIONS

We designed the questionnaire along the chronological sequence of an acquisition program. To avoid repetition, we shall use *mergers* and *acquisitions* interchangeably to mean *a form of marriage* without concern with legal distinction. The first event is the decision to use acquisitions as a means for the firm's growth. We sought to obtain information about the reasons which motivated the management and the strategy employed. We particularly sought to classify behavior into typical strategy classes: horizontal mergers, vertical, concentric, and conglomerate.

The second major question of concern was the degree of pre-planning for carrying out the strategy: (a) To what extent did the firm specifically identify the objectives, the strategy, and developed criteria for analysis of alternatives?

We called this the strategic or "when-to" type of planning. A question of current interest was the extent to which firms pursued related synergistic acquisitions, as opposed to unrelated conglomerate ones. (b) Did the firm establish procedures for search, allocate specific responsibilities and budgets for the conduct of the acquisition search and evaluation? We called this operational or "how-to" planning.

The third major question dealt with the actual manner of search used, the procedures for evaluation, the thoroughness, and the ratio of candidates to final closures, etc.

The fourth area of concern was the post-acquisition activities: the degree of integration between the parent and subsidiary firms, the responsibilities of the respective parties in effecting the marriage. We were particularly interested in the degree of synergy realized and the types of problems encountered in the assimilation process.

Finally, we asked the responding firms their estimates of the over-all success: The degree to which the firm's acquisition objectives were met.

A copy of the questionnaire can be found in Appendix A. The questionnaire was mailed to 412 firms. Ninety-three usable responses were received. The following results are based on this sample.

HOW DO FIRMS CONDUCT MERGERS?–THE ANSWERS

We offered the responders nineteen different possible reasons for engaging in acquisition activities and invited them to rank their respective importance in the firm's program, as well as all reasons of their own. Their responses indicate that major importance was attached to rounding out of product lines and to increased market penetration. Use of firm's marketing capabilities, offsetting unsatisfactory growth prospects, and use of distinctive technological expertise of the parent were the second most high-ranking groups of reasons.

Interestingly, a desire to utilize idle production capacity, frequently the trigger for interest in mergers, ranked a low eighth in terms of the ultimate reasons for pursuing them.

Very much in line with these objectives were the respective strategies of the firms. Horizontal strategy of rounding out the product line and concentric strategy of seeking synergistic common threads were reported in 68% of the acquisitions. The conglomerate strategy of unrelated acquisition motivated only 19% of our sample. These percentages should not be interpreted as representing a random sample for acquisitions during the period. As explained in Chapter 2, there are several biases necessary to our sampling process.

One of the most conclusive and interesting results concerned planning. The respondents quite sharply polarized themselves into "planners" and "non-planners." The planners generally engaged in both "when-to" and "how-to" planning and conducted well-organized and well-directed programs of search and evaluation. If they planned at all, they not only planned the full range, but also implemented their plans in a systematic manner. On the other hand, nonplanners tended to forego planning altogether and, with it, systematic management of the acquisition process.

When asked about their perception of the success of the merger programs, about 70% of nonplanners felt that their objectives were met, compared with 86% for firms which engaged in complete and thorough planning. A possible explanation for a surprisingly small difference may lie in the fact that the nonplanners, having set no objectives in the first place, were less critical of their own performance than the planners. This hypothesis will be supported later when we discuss a comparison of questionnaires and financial results.

In the conduct of acquisitions, only 29% of the firms took a passive approach of waiting for opportunities to come along. The remaining 70% either let it be generally known what they wanted, or identified and pursued opportunities of their own choice. A significant result is that, of the candidates whose acquisitions were consummated, 69% of the initial contacts were made directly by the acquiring firms and not by an intermediary.

Considering the importance of acquisitions to the firm's future performance, a surprisingly small resource was allocated to the acquisition activity. Only 14% of the firms took the trouble to set up a formal acquisitions activity budget. The number of people in any one firm with full-time responsibilities for acquisition ranged from one to six. The average for our sample was just below one. The number of preliminary screenings varied from two to six. On the average, for every consummated acquisition, 1.5 were thoroughly evaluated, using one man-month of effort. The typical length of consummation, from identification to closure, was about ten months.

In the total sample, 35% of the firms experienced one or more post-acquisition problems. The occurrence of the problems is strongly related to the responsibilities which the *acquired* firm was given for the integration process. When the acquired firm was given no voice, 92% experienced problems; on the other hand, with equally shared responsibilities, only 28% had problems.

As would be expected, acquiring firms with conglomerate strategy usually attempted little integration and, as a result, experienced fewer problems (30% of the cases for conglomerates, compared to 66% for synergistic mergers).

On the other hand, attainment of synergy was directly related to the degree of integration used. Since 76% of the firms sought one or another form of synergy, this was deemed an important consideration. Only 58% of acquisitions attained synergy when the acquired firm was given an autonomous status, while 76% attainment occurred under conditions of complete integration.

Planning (of the "how-to" variety) also was important in attainment of synergy; 64% of firms which sought synergy *and* planned did, in fact, attain it, while only 57% of those who didn't plan obtained synergy.

In judging their own estimates of the over-all results, acquiring firms felt that about 20% of acquisitions were considered outright failures, 21% were a full success, the remaining 59% were judged a partial success.

One of the most conclusive relationships of the study is the correlation of the attainment of synergy and the perceived accomplishment of objectives. Virtually all firms which attained synergy considered themselves successful, while only 60% of the firms which sought but failed to get-synergy felt that most of their objectives were met.

DO MERGERS SUCCEED?—THE QUESTIONS

In addition to eliciting subjective estimates of success by the firms themselves, we performed a detailed quantitative analysis of merger results. As a source of data, we used Standard and Poor's Compustat Tapes which contain all relevant financial data on some 900 firms for the period 1946-1965.

In order to evaluate the results of merger activity, we wanted to compare the change that took place in the firm from a pre- to a post-merger period. To this end, we defined an "acquisition program" which consisted of four years of merger-free activity, followed by a period of at least one merger at least every other year, followed by two years of merger-free activity. Application of these rules reduced the Compustat sample to 271 firms which had at least one acceptable merger program. The results reported below are all based on this sample.

For measurement of results we chose thirteen different financial measures. These are shown in Table 1-1. These were computed in three ways: For some, we used an average of annual growth rates (Class I); for some, average growth rate over a period (Class II); and for some, an average value during a period (Class III). These are defined in Table 1-1. Class I and Class II are complementary ways of measuring growth characteristics, while Class III measures the average position of the firm before and after acquisition.

Previous studies had indicated that merging firms as a class do not do significantly better than a total population of firms. We wanted to check this

TABLE 1-1

VARIABLES CALCULATED IN STUDY

Variable	Type Measure		
	I	II	III
Sales	X	X	
Earnings	X	X	
Earnings/Share	X	X	
Total Assets	X	X	
Earnings/Equity	X	X	
Dividends/Share		X	
Stock Price (Adjusted)		X	
Debt/Equity		X	X
Common Equity		X	X
Earnings/Total Equity		X	X
Price/Earnings Ratio (Adjusted)			X
Payout (Dividends/Earnings)			X
Price/Equity Ratio			X
TOTAL	5	10	6

Type Measures

I.   Average of annual percentage growth

$$\frac{100}{N} \sum_{t=1}^{N} \frac{X_t - X_{t-1}}{X_{t-1}}$$

Where N = number of years in period and X_t = value of variable in t^{th} year of period.

II.   Average percentage change over period

$$\frac{100}{N} \frac{X_N - X_1}{X_1}$$

III.   Average value over period

$$\frac{1}{N} \sum_{t=1}^{N} X_t$$

result, but we also wanted to see whether there were differences in performance *within* the sample of acquisitions. With this in mind, we divided the sample into three subclasses according to pre-acquisition growth rates in sales: a slow-growth class with less than 4% growth rate, a medium class with 4% to 10%, and fast growers with more than 10%. We made similar subdivisions according to earnings growth, pre-acquisition size of the firm, and the number of acquisitions made during the program.

Using the above performance measures and the classifications, we made three distinctive comparisons: (1) confining our attention to the sample of acquiring firms (271 mentioned above), we studied their respective pre- and post-acquisition performance; (2) we next compared pre- and post-acquisition performance between acquirers and firms which grew exclusively by internal expansion; (3) as a final measure, we compared performance traces of acquirers to nonacquirers over the entire 20-year history contained in the Compustat tapes.

DO MERGERS SUCCEED?—THE ANSWERS

(a)   *Comparison of Pre- and Post-Acquisition Performance*

For virtually every significant growth characteristic (Class I and Class II in Table 1-1), the low-sales-growth firms show impressively higher growth rates during the post-acquisition than during the pre-acquisition period. This is illustrated in Figure 1-1 (more detailed comparisons will be found in Chapter 3).

As seen in Figure 1-1, the firms with initially high growth show the opposite effect of declining growth rates as a result of acquisitions.

However, when pre- and post-acquisition positions (rather than growth rates) are compared, a reversal of roles takes place. This is illustrated in Figure 1-2. Here the improvements accrue to the high-growth firms, and low-growth firms decline. This effect holds for most Class III variables as can be seen in Chapter 4. A significant exception is in the measure of efficiency in the use of employed capital. On this measure, *all* growth classes did worse after acquisitions.

Thus it appears that there was a trade-off in accomplishment: high-growth firms suffered a loss in growth characteristics, but improved their position; low-growth firms improved their growth characteristics at the expense of position variables. It is interesting to note (see Figure 1-2) that the market did not reward the low-growth firms for their search of a growth image—their price/earnings ratios on the average declined. On the other hand, the high growers' price/earnings ratios increased after acquisition.

Another result of interest is that low-growth firms appeared to finance their acquisitions through decreased dividend payout and new debt, while fast growers actually decreased their debt/equity ratios and increased dividend payout.

When the total sample was sliced into subclasses according to pre-acquisition earnings (rather than sales) growth, virtually the same results were obtained. Using the number of acquisitions per firm as the ordering variable shows no significant differences between active and less active acquirers.

A very interesting result is obtained when the sample is sliced according to

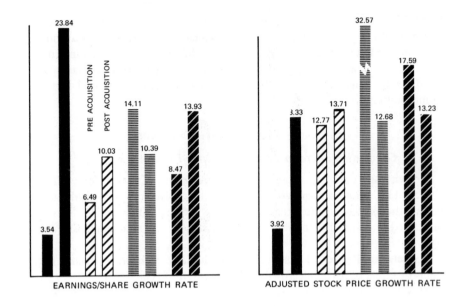

EARNINGS/SHARE GROWTH RATE

ADJUSTED STOCK PRICE GROWTH RATE

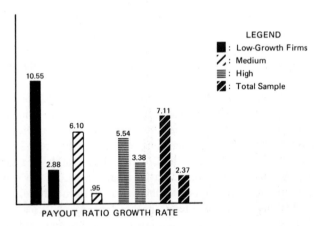

PAYOUT RATIO GROWTH RATE

LEGEND
■ : Low-Growth Firms
▨ : Medium
▤ : High
▨ : Total Sample

Fig. 1-1.
Comparison of Pre- and Post-Acquisition
Growth Rates (by Growth Class).

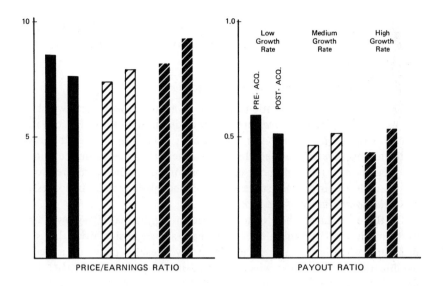

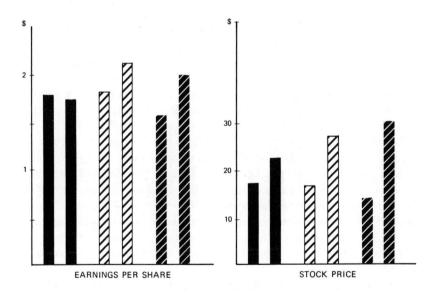

Fig. 1-2.
Comparison of Pre- and Post-Acquisition
Mean Performance Values (by Growth Class).

11

the size of the acquirer. Small firms behave much like slow-growth firms, but large ones (sales greater than $100 million) do significantly better than high-growth firms.

(b)   *Comparison of Acquiring to Nonacquiring Firms*

Comparison of pre-acquisition behavior of acquirers with firms which did not use acquisitions as a growth method provided insights into the motivation behind acquisitions. Results for slow-growth firms suggest that they were motivated by adversity: either a history of deteriorating performance prior to the program or a relatively poor current performance when compared to the total sample of firms. This suggests the "problemistic search" hypothesis in *The Behavioral Theory of the Firm.* [1]

On the other hand, there is no evidence to suggest that high-growth firms were motivated by anything other than an aggressive drive by their management to grow and excel. These two results point to a needed modification of viewpoint which is found in many studies of *"the"* firm: firms differ in their responses, largely due to the differences of managerial motivation. Therefore, significant new insights may be gathered, if studies were to stratify the population of firms into significant subclasses.

By constructing artificial pre- and post-acquisition periods for the nonacquiring firms (see Chapter 4 for detail), we were able to compare their *increments* in pre- to post-acquisition performance to those of the acquirers. This is illustrated in Table 1-2.

The first seven columns which compare growth rates give a generally unfavorable picture of the acquiring firms, with the exception of earnings on total capital and earnings on equity for the slow-growth firms. The last three columns are inconclusive and certainly would not lead one to conclude that mergers are a superior method of growth unless the very strong performance of high growers on price/earnings ratios is taken as the dominant criterion.

When the total sample is considered, this conclusion is supported by the 20-year history shown in the lower right-hand corner of Figure 1-3; on the other hand, we again see reversals between classes: slow-growth firms had a poorer net result in growth of earnings per share and high-growth firms came out ahead, although they lagged behind the nonacquirers through most of the period.

Finally, but importantly, the acquiring firms held an unmistakable edge on nonacquirers in earnings on total capital. During the 20-year period, the

[1] Richard M. Cyert and James G. March, *A Behavioral Theory of the Firm* (Englewood Cliffs, N.J.: Prentice-Hall, 1963), p. 46.

TABLE 1-2

COMPARATIVE CHANGES IN VARIABLES BETWEEN
PRE- AND POST-ACQUISITION PERIODS

	LOW GROWTH	MEDIUM GROWTH	HIGH GROWTH	ALL FIRMS
RATIO OF CHANGE IN GROWTH RATES				
Sales	.69	.18	(-) 1.26	(-) 1.42
Earnings	.97	.12	$\frac{-13.50}{+6.50}$	.19
Earnings/Share	.86	.12	$\frac{-10.34}{+7.68}$	.22
Stock Price	.28	.03	$\frac{-19.89}{+2.71}$	$\frac{-4.36}{(-) 22.52}$
Earnings/Total Capital	2.10	.22	$\frac{-2.36}{+2.14}$	.77
Earnings/Common Equity	2.32	.26	$\frac{-2.19}{+.10}$	1.06
Total Debt/Equity	.67	.27	(-).73	(-).19
RATIOS OF AVERAGE VALUES				
Price/Earnings	(-).52	$\frac{.65}{-2.04}$	1.59	$\frac{+.35}{-.70}$
Price/Equity	1.28	2.09	.99	1.07
Earnings/Total Capital	(-) 1.00	(-) 1.00	(-) 1.00	(-) 1.00

secular trend has been downward, as shown in Figure 1-3. However, the acquiring firms have been much more successful in arresting this trend.

DOES PLANNING PAY?

A polarization of the questionnaire answers into "planners" and "nonplanners" has made it possible for us to determine whether planning contributes to success of acquisitions.

Three tests were performed: (1) a correlation analysis between individual planning activities and the resulting increment in the firm's performance; (2) a statistical comparison of performance of "ideal planners" as a group against the "nonplanners". (It will be recalled that questionnaire replies made this possible by indicating clear polarization of planners against nonplanners.) (3)

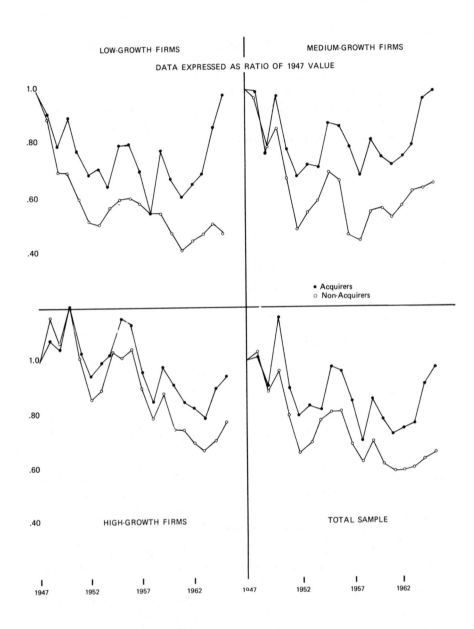

LOW-GROWTH FIRMS

MEDIUM-GROWTH FIRMS

DATA EXPRESSED AS RATIO OF 1947 VALUE

• Acquirers
○ Non-Acquirers

HIGH-GROWTH FIRMS

TOTAL SAMPLE

1947   1952   1957   1962   1947   1952   1957   1962

Fig. 1-3
Comparative Growth, Acquirers and Nonacquirers,
on Earnings/Total Capital Ratio.

14

a graphical comparison of the distributions of performance on all significant variables.

The correlation analysis (see Table 5-1 in Chapter 5) showed a strong correlation between individual planning attributes and improvement in performance. The statistical comparison which is given in Table 1-3 shows that the mean performance improvement of the "ideal" planners clearly dominates that of nonplanners. Further, the performance of the planners is more predictable, as indicated by smaller standard deviations.

There is one exception: the ideal planners did poorer on improvement in the price/earnings ratio, which indicates that the investing public either lacked the data or was unwilling to give credit for the superior performance of the planners.

The complete distributions, one of which is shown in Figure 1-4, further support this conclusion.

Thus all tests point strongly to the conclusion that planners performed better and more predictably than did nonplanners.

TABLE 1-3

COMPARISON OF MEANS AND STANDARD DEVIATIONS OF PERFORMANCE MEASURES FOR "IDEAL" FIRMS AND THOSE WITH RANDOM BEHAVIOR

	MEANS		STANDARD DEVIATIONS	
	Ideal Firms	Other	Ideal Firms	Other
Sales Growth Rate Change I	2.75	-.63	12.62	9.25
Earnings Growth Rate Change I	13.14	10.86	31.62	45.13
Earnings/Share Growth Rate Change I	12.83	9.98	32.44	44.01
Total Assets Growth Rate Change I	-.64	.57	6.42	8.54
Earnings/Common Equity Growth Rate Change I	11.39	10.52	28.63	40.21
Sales Growth Rate Change II	-.82	-11.18	17.91	24.60
Earnings Growth Rate Change II	13.61	2.03	32.33	72.10
Earnings/Share Growth Rate Change II	14.01	1.79	30.28	68.06
Total Assets Growth Rate Change II	-5.16	-8.93	13.05	25.68
Earnings/Common Equity Growth Rate Change II	12.28	8.45	21.68	54.63
Payout Ratio Growth Rate Change II	-3.34	-.3.80	14.96	27.77
Total Equity Growth Rate Change II	-1.22	-7.61	7.86	15.33
Earnings/Total Capital Growth Rate Change II	12.80	7.15	24.47	50.91
Adjusted Stock Price Growth Rate Change II	7.77	-10.42	32.53	45.21
Debt/Equity Growth Rate Change II	-6.00	-1.85	16.79	18.86
Price/Earnings Ratio Change III	-.16	2.07	2.29	5.54
Debt/Equity Ratio Change III	0.00	-0.10	0.17	0.27
Payout Ratio Change III	-0.02	0.15	0.14	0.60
Price/Equity Ratio Change III	0.70	0.80	0.91	0.94
Total Equity Change III	58.91	67.77	95.65	127.34
Earnings/Total Equity Ratio Change III	-0.02	-0.03	0.04	0.04

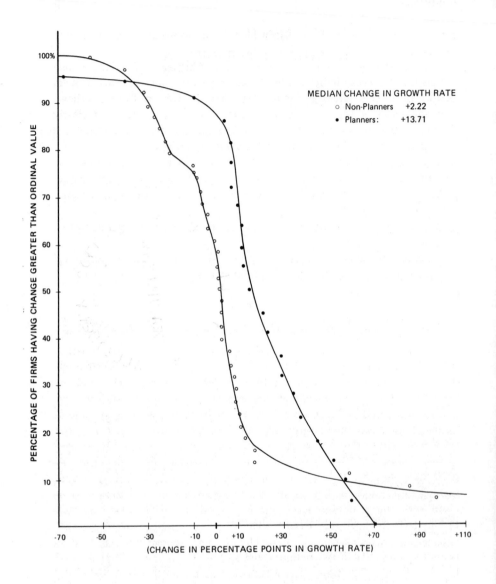

Fig. 1-4.
Comparative Distribution of Change in
Growth Rate of Earnings/Share between
Planners and Nonplanners

CHAPTER 2

THE STUDY IN PERSPECTIVE

The purpose of this study was to examine the efficacy of merging and acquiring as means to corporate growth. Areas of interest in the study included the performance averages for those firms that used mergers and acquisitions instead of internal development, the range of such performances, and the reasons why some firms following the acquisition route were successful while others were not. This chapter examines the research methodologies, the characteristics of the firm sampled, and selected other relevant studies in the recent literature.

SECTION 1: RESEARCH METHODOLOGIES AND SAMPLES OF FIRMS STUDIED

The Standard and Poor Compustat tapes have provided researchers with a significant machine-readable data base for much of the public financial information on a large sample of firms. As might be expected, a rash of research followed, manipulating this data base to provide statistics on performance (defined in a variety of ways) of industries, market indices, mutual funds, and various groupings of firms. In most investigations, the method of setting up the samples implied some form of common management behavior which was a significant factor in causing the sample firms to perform as they did. For example, one study inferred that top managers were making acquisitions with a resulting increase in size of firm (measured in assets and number of employees) and were motivated to improve their own self-interest to a greater extent than they were motivated to increase stockholder benefits (measured in dividends, stock appreciation, etc.). After reviewing a number of these studies, the authors felt that more insight could be gained if data on managerial practices were obtained directly from the firms (and not imputed by researchers) and then combined with objective performance measures available with the use of the Compustat tapes. Consequently, this study used computer programs to analyze the financial data on a variety of measures for groupings of firms classified on several pertinent dimensions (such as growth rate or the number of acquisitions).

17

Because there are so many unspecified factors that can affect a firm's performance, a large sample size was considered necessary. The Compustat tapes easily provide the objective data for a large sample. Field interviews, however, would be too costly to permit extensive data gathering on the same sample. Recognizing the disadvantages of questionnaire studies (including potentially low response rates and response biases in this case), the investigators still felt that more data could be gathered with greater comparability if questionnaires were used. The construction, pre-testing, mailing and analysis of the questionnaires is discussed in the next chapter. It is worth noting here, however, that questionnaires were divided into two parts to take advantage of the perceptions of managers who participated in the acquisition activities and to make use of the formal record system of the firm. Because many of the acquisitions which we studied occurred more than five years prior to the investigation, intensive field research still would have been limited to incomplete formal records within the firm. The first section of the questionnaire relies on the memory of an executive intimately involved in the acquisition process. The second section was designed for completion by a staff analyst in the firm using the formal records.

The questionnaire was mailed to 412 manufacturing firms which had at least one acquisition during the period 1946-1965. By restricting the study to manufacturing firms we made the economic climate, legal restraints, etc., more similar throughout the sample than would have been the case if banks and other institutions had been included. The 412 firms were identified by a search program on the Compustat tapes.

Because we wanted to compare the performance of firms before and after an acquisition or series of acquisitions, the sample of 412 firms was reduced to 271 firms that had a sufficient period of time before and after their acquisition programs to permit such comparison. The detailed rationale and method of selecting these pre- and post-acquisition periods is explained in Chapter 4, Section 1. Because firms pursuing a conglomerate acquisition strategy rarely had significant periods of time without acquisitions, our sample of 271 firms included a smaller proportion of conglomerates than would be found in the total acquisition movement. There were still, however, a significant number of firms in the sample which reported a conglomerate strategy as the motivation for their acquisition activity.

Another set of performance reference standards was constructed by selecting a sample of nonacquiring firms with approximately the same characteristics as the sample of 271 acquiring firms. This sample of 82 nonacquiring firms was made up of manufacturing firms listed on the Compustat tapes which had a 20-year history of data and no acquisitions from 1946-1965. The characteristics of this sample were quite similar to those of the 271 acquiring firms, with the possible exception of a larger average equity base for the nonacquiring sample. Characteristics of each sample are delineated in Chapter 4.

The questionnaire return yielded 93 usable responses from firms which had acquired a total of 299 other firms. The findings presented in Chapter 3 on the practices of management during acquisition activities are based on information on these 93 companies. Of these 93 responses, 62 firms also were included in the sample of 271 firms for which objective performance data were available. Thus, for 62 firms, relationships could be studied among a number of features of management decision processes, individual firms' perception of their own successes (Chapter 3), and more objective performance measures (Chapter 5). This sample of 62 firms demonstrated one of the most significant results of the study: that certain planning practices are highly correlated with success as measured by standard financial criteria. This conclusion is based on the comparison of two groups of the sample of 62 firms: 22 firms which were categorized as "ideal" planners on the basis of planning practices, and 40 firms that did little formal planning of their acquisition activities.

In order that the reader may judge how representative our samples are of the population containing all of those firms involved in acquisitions and mergers, several characteristics are described below and compared to a larger sample in a comprehensive study made by the Federal Trade Commission. The relative sizes of acquiring firms and those firms which were acquired are particularly important in judging the validity of the results reported in Chapter 5. Figures 2-1 and 2-2 show, respectively, the distributions of relative asset sizes and sales between acquirer and acquired firm. In most cases, the acquisition represented a very sizable increase in the assets and sales of the acquirer. Had the majority of the acquisitions been very small in comparison to the acquiring firm, the correlations between certain management practices and firm performance would have been suspect because the acquisition event might easily have had inconsequential effects compared to other events such as strikes, new product development, or general economic conditions.

The number of acquisitions in an acquisition program did not have an obvious effect on the relative size of acquisitions sought by the acquirer. Figures 2-3 and 2-4 show that the average ratio of sizes (acquired firm to acquirer) is not highly correlated to the total number of acquisitions which the acquirer consummated in its acquisition program.

Further evidence that the firms investigated in this study do not comprise a biased sample from the total population of acquiring firms is presented in

Assets of Acquired \ Assets of Acquirer	1-10	10-20	20-50	50-100	100-500	>500
0-1			4	5	1	3
1-5	2	3	5	9	6	4
5-10	1	1	1	6	5	1
10-20		1	5	5	17	6
20-50		2		4	9	7
50-100					4	3
>100					4	5

Fig. 2-1.
Assets Distribution Matrix of Individual Acquisitions.
(Assets in million $)

Acquired \ Acquirer		1-10	10-20	20-50	50-100	100-500	>500
0-1	0-1						
1-5	1-5	2	1	1		8	
5-10	5-10		1	1	4	6	2
	10-20		1	2	4	11	4
	20-50			1	5	18	9
	50-100			1,		5	4
	>100					3	7

Fig. 2-2.
Sales Distribution Matrix of Individual Acquisitions.
(Sales in million $)

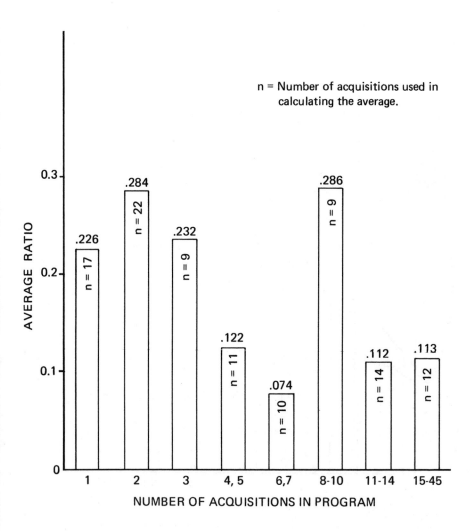

Fig. 2-3.
Average Ratios of Asset Size—Acquired Firm to Acquirer—Depending
upon the Number of Acquisitions in the Program.

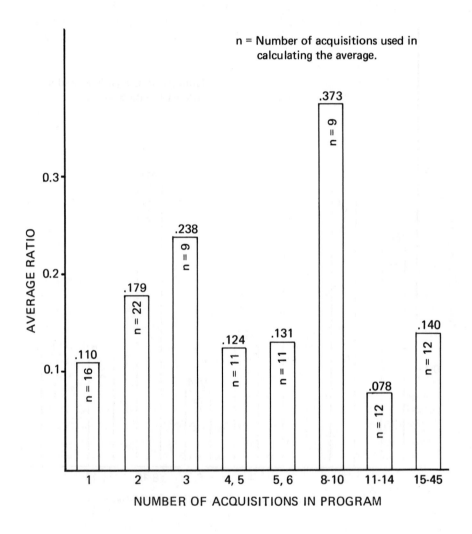

n = Number of acquisitions used in calculating the average.

AVERAGE RATIO

.373
n = 9

.238
n = 9

.179
n = 22

.140
n = 12

.131
n = 11

.124
n = 11

.110
n = 16

.078
n = 12

0.3

0.2

0.1

1   2   3   4, 5   5, 6   8-10   11-14   15-45

NUMBER OF ACQUISITIONS IN PROGRAM

Fig. 2-4.
Average Sales Ratios—Acquired Firm to Acquirer—Depending
upon the Number of Acquisitions in the Program.

Figure 2-5. This figure compares the asset size class of acquiring firms examined in this study to firms investigated in a comprehensive study, *Economic Repört on Corporate Mergers,* published in 1969 by the Federal Trade Commission. The F.T.C. survey included 1,276 acquisitions. The main difference between the two samples is that a higher percentage of very large acquirers is included in the F.T.C. survey.

SECTION 2: EVIDENCE FROM OTHER RELATED STUDIES

In general, the literature on mergers and acquisitions is primarily focused on conglomerate-growth firms. Several articles have analyzed conglomerates with respect to their legal apsects, public policy effects, implications for economic theory, and portfolio theory. Empirical studies are few in number.

To place this investigation in perspective, the work of selected researchers is outlined here. This work is illustrative of other methods and types of analyses which have been made of merger and acquisition behavior.

Two studies focused on the economic performance of conglomerates.[1] In the first, performance of sixty conglomerates during 1958-67 is analyzed, on measures of sales, net income, total assets, earnings per share growth, average market price growth, and price earnings ratio. Performance was compared with averages for all manufacturing firms during the same period. The results of both showed that conglomerates grew faster than other industrials and that they were nearly as profitable (the difference not being significant). The general conclusion was that conglomerate firms have performed satisfactorily.

Another study compared conglomerates with other types of mergers.[2] Horizontal, vertical, and concentric mergers performed worse than the conglomerates and internal-growth firms on measures of profitability and growth. When Reid did not consider the merger type, he found that internal-growth firms were more profitable than acquirers, but their growth performance was less. From these results, Reid concluded that internal-growth firms tend to further the self-interest of the stockholders, while the more a firm acquires, the more it tends to further the self-interests of its management.

[1] Fred J. Weston, "Diversification and Merger Trends," *Business Economics,* V, No. 1 (January 1970), 50-57; Fred J. Weston and Surendra K. Mansinghka, "Tests of the Efficiency Performance of Conglomerate Firms" (working paper).

[2] Samuel R. Reid, *Mergers, Managers, and the Economy* (New York: McGraw-Hill, 1968).

Asset size class of acquiring company (million $)	This Study		F.T.C. Study[1]	
	Number of Acquisitions	% of total Acquisitions	Number of Acquisitions	% of total Acquisitions
250 and over	185	25.1	473	37.1
100-250	174	23.7	307	24.1
50-100	152	20.7	187	14.7
25-50	104	14.1	157	12.3
10-25	85	11.5	105	8.2
under 10	36	4.9	47	3.7
Total	736	100.0	1276	100.0

[1]From F.T.C. study, *Economic Report on Corporate Mergers* (New York: Commerce Clearing House, 1969), p. A-8.
The F.T.C. study, however, considers only acquisitions of $10 million or more in assets over the period 1948-68.

Fig. 2-5.
Comparison of Size Distribution of Acquiring Company:
this Study vs. Federal Trade Commission Study.

Qualitative Studies. A study by Kitching deals with the factors that cause acquisition programs to be successful or unsuccessful.[3] Top executives of 22 companies were interviewed on their views of the success or failure of acquisitions compared to original strategies and on source of payoff from acquisitions. The evidence from these interviews points to strategic planning as the major factor in successful acquisition programs. But Kitching says that a more important factor is having enough "managers of change" ("who could take an unplanned acquisition whose resources are related only indirectly to those of the parent company and make a success of it.")

[3] John Kitching, "Why Do Mergers Miscarry," *Harvard Business Review*, XLV, No. 6 (November-December 1967), 84-101.

CHAPTER 3

MANAGEMENT APPROACH TO ACQUISITIONS

This chapter concentrates on investigating the motivation and acquisition behavior of acquiring firms. Early in the study we hypothesized that different modes of managerial behavior should lead to different results. In particular, we expected that there should be significant differences between the firms which approached these programs in a planned and systematic manner, as opposed to firms which took an ad hoc approach.

To test this hypothesis, we designed and mailed a questionnaire to all the firms indicating at least one acquisition in the period 1946-65. The returns were first analyzed for insights which they offered about differences among acquisition behavior of firms. When these results were combined with the financial performance, it was then possible to compare the objective outcomes of different modes of managerial behavior.

This process is described in the next two sections: Section 1 describes the questionnaire and the data collection process, and Section 2 presents the results of the questionnaire study.

SECTION 1: DESIGN OF THE QUESTIONNAIRE AND DATA COLLECTION METHOD

Questionnaire Design. The questionnaire, which is presented at the end of this section, was written in two different forms. Although the same general information was sought on both forms, the format of one form was pertinent to acquisition programs with a single acquisition, while the other form pertained to multiple-acquisition programs.

We sought to enhance the probability of response and the obtaining of valid data by personalizing the cover letter and the questionnaire. The questionnaire was addressed to an executive of the firm who would be most likely to have had direct involvement in the acquisition program. Whenever possible, the questionnaires were mailed directly to executives who had previous association with the investigators. The questionnaire contained the names and dates of acquisitions to identify the program under investigation to the respondent.

Each questionnaire was divided into two sections: the first seeking subjective evaluations of the acquisition activity, and the second requesting objective information from company records. We requested that the first part be completed by someone who was directly involved in the concerned acquisition program. We suggested that the second part be completed by a staff analyst.

For most questions, checklists of alternative answers were presented in order to minimize the time required of the respondent. The investigators felt that the possible disadvantage of restricting the range of answers was more than offset by the increased probability of response and the ease of coding the data.

To test the validity of the data, several checks for consistency were built into the questionnaire. Inconsistencies were noted in only 2% of the responses. There was also little evidence of a post-decision rationalization process which would invalidate the analysis. Many respondents quite frankly expressed dissatisfaction with their acquisition process. Of course, each respondent was assured that his reply would be treated as highly confidential to encourage realistic disclosure.

The questionnaire was pretested by having four executives complete it in the presence of an investigator. Each executive was requested to ignore the investigator until he had completed the questionnaire but to note any ambiguities he had discovered. Two of the executives were from the same company so that the reliability of the questionnaire could be tested. In this case, four of the forty-one questions had discrepancies in the answers. In all cases, the discrepancies were so minor that it was possible to rephrase two of the questions to remove some of the difficulties. The time required to complete both parts of the questionnaire ranged from about twenty to thirty-five minutes. In one instance, however, the requested financial figures could not be supplied without considerable delay. Comments from the executives were extremely helpful in making the questionnaire more readable and reliable.

Collection of Data. A sample mailing was made to 65 firms having single-acquisition programs. If the investigators had no previous association with an executive of a firm to which a questionnaire was sent, the questionnaire was addressed to a vice-president of corporate planning or corporate development or to an executive vice-president. The sample mailing had a response rate of 23% and there was no evidence of inconsistencies or invalid response, nor were there any adverse comments on the format from the respondents.

An additional 347 questionnaires were mailed to complete the survey of 412 firms that are listed on the Standard and Poor Compustat tapes and for which appropriate acquisition programs had been identified. A total of 93 firms responded. These 93 firms had acquired 299 other firms during the acquisition programs under investigation. This response rate of 22.6% is very favorable, considering the proprietary nature of the information sought, the workload of the respondents (usually vice-presidents), and the fact that, in some cases, information was requested on programs that had occurred ten to fifteen years ago.

The majority of firms that did not complete the questionnaire did send a letter of explanation. For this reason, a second questionnaire which the investigators had planned to send, in order to check for nonresponse bias, was not mailed. There were two common reasons for not responding. The most common was simply that the information was no longer available even to the firm. This typically occurred when the merger program was more than ten years before the questionnaire mailing. In these cases, the person in charge of or knowing the most about the acquisition activities had left the firm and his replacement disqualified himself as not having sufficient information. In more than 70% of the responses, the person to whom the questionnaire was addressed replied that he personally completed at least the first segment. This success is crucial to the study. It is the primary reason why the additional effort was made to secure a mailing list which included, as much as possible, people who had had previous contact with the investigators through consulting, management seminars, and other presentations. For this reason, the investigators are confident that the responses were usually made by people whose perceptions of the planning process would be most accurate and valid.

The second reason for lack of response was that one or more of the acquisitions had caused the acquiring firm to be scrutinized for possible violation of antitrust legislation. Firms in this position acknowledged a hesitancy to provide information to anyone. (In two cases, the acquiring firms had been forced to divest the acquisitions, causing the acquisition programs to be invalid for our investigation.)

Our subsample of firms that did respond, therefore, might possibly include a slight bias on two dimensions. The acquisition behavior of firms which responded to our questionnaire is more likely to be representative of recent acquisition behavior of firms which were not scrutinized for possible antitrust violations. However, it is the opinion of the investigators that these possible biases are slight and unlikely to affect significantly the results of this study. The reason is that there is no evidence of significant differences between the behavior of responding firms with older programs and those with newer programs, or responding firms which reported antitrust action and those which did not.

A copy of the complete questionnaire is provided in Appendix A.

SECTION 2: THE RESULTS OF THE QUESTIONNAIRE STUDY

The results of the questionnaire are used in this study in two ways. First, the responses provided us with insight into the acquisition practices of a broad sample of firms. (All 93 respondents were used for this purpose.) This acquisition behavior will be examined in the following discussion. Second, when coupled with financial performance measures of the firm before and after acquiring, the questionnaire data provided us with insights into the relationship between different approaches to acquisition activity and their financial success or failure. (Sixty of the respondents coincided with the firms for which we had objective financial data and, hence, were used for this purpose.) These findings are discussed in Chapter 4.

Acquisition Strategies. The firms in this study undertook acquisition programs with a wide variety of objectives. Almost all of the responding firms ranked a multiplicity of reasons according to their relative importance in each of the acquisition programs. Table 3-1 shows weighted rankings of the various reasons for acquiring. The most important reason on each response was assigned five points, with less important reasons receiving progressively fewer points. The total points for each reason, accumulated for all responses, are shown in the table. It is interesting to observe that, despite the publicity given to conglomerate merger activity during the latter part of our study period, a majority of the acquiring firms put high emphasis on the relationship between the products, markets, and technologies of the merging firms.

This observation is supported by the relative frequency of diversification types (horizontal, vertical, concentric, or conglomerate) sought by the acquiring firm. (In most cases with multiple-acquisition programs, the diversification strategy remained the same throughout the program. Thus, respondents generally provided a single descriptor for the entire program.) Of responding firms, 33% of the acquisitions were horizontal; that is, the acquired firm and the acquiring firm were in the same industry and had similar markets. About 13% of the acquisitions were vertical: the acquired firms were customers or suppliers of the acquiring firms. Concentric diversification, where both firms have the same markets but different

TABLE 3-1

THE RELATIVE IMPORTANCE OF REASONS FOR ACQUIRING

Reason	Points
1) To complete product lines	159
2) To increase market share	102
3) To fully utilize existing marketing capabilities, contacts, or channels	73
4) To offset unsatisfactory sales growth in present market	70
5) To capitalize on distinctive technological expertise	64
6) To obtain patents, licenses, or technological know-how	53
7) To meet demand of diversified customers	45
8) To fully utilize existing production capacity	43
9) To increase control of sales outlets	39
10) To reduce dependence on suppliers	38
11) To reduce dependence on one or few customers	34
12) To acquire goodwill, prestige, or brand names	30
13) To capitalize on distinctive managerial talents	30
14) To offset unsatisfactory profit margins in present markets	26
15) To attain a minimum size needed for efficient research and development	7
16) To attain a minimum size needed for effective advertising methods	3
17) To attain a minimum size needed for listing on stock exchange	1
18) To utilize waste or by-products	1
19) To offset technological obsolescence of facilities	0

technologies and products, occurred in 35% of the acquisition programs. An example of this type of acquisition would be a can company purchasing a firm whose major product line is plastic containers. Only 19% of the acquisition programs had a conglomerate diversification strategy; that is, neither the markets nor the technologies were the same for the acquiring and acquired firms. However, because of our definition of acquisition programs, firms with conglomerate diversification strategies were less likely to have been included in our study. Consequently, the percentage of firms seeking conglomerate acquisitions is probably lower for our sample than it would be for acquiring firms in general. Later sections of this chapter will relate differences in performance and methods of acquisition to these different diversification strategies.

Planning the Acquisition Activity. Two different types of acquisition planning behavior were studied. The first type is strategic "when-to" planning for determining if and when the firm should seek acquisitions. Such planning may result in policies requiring continuous scanning for opportunities, or in rules for initiating activity when a particular type of opportunity or threat to the firm occurs. Such planning typically includes an explicit statement and ranking of corporate objectives. Data used to categorize firms on this dimension came from questions 1, 2, 3, 4, 7, and 8 on the first part of the questionnaire. This type of planning also usually identifies the strategy for improving performance. For example, these methods may include acquiring other firms, expanding market promotions, or heavier investment in basic and applied research. Information gathered from the responses to questions 5, 6, and 8 (Part I) provided insight on this type of behavior.

The second type of planning is "how-to," or operational planning of the mechanisms for acquiring, given that the firm has already decided that it desires to acquire and what is to be accomplished by the acquisition program. This type of planning is evidenced by establishing procedures for searching for candidates, standards for their evaluation, and allocation of specific budgets in support of the acquisition activity. Firms were categorized on their extent of "how-to" planning using data from questions 9-15, Part I, and 3-7, Part II.

In spite of the growing number of firms who are considering mergers and acquisitions, our results suggest that, on the whole, in the last decade, there has been no increase in the percentage of firms who plan. Table 3-2 shows that there has not been a significant increase in the degree of planning, although the raw data in the table suggests a trend toward greater use of planning (compare columns 1 and 4). The null hypothesis (the distribution of planning before 1960 is the same as after 1960) is accepted at the 0.25 level of significance using the chi-square goodness-of-fit test.

Responses clearly show that, when a firm engaged in "when-to" planning, it was very likely also to have used "how-to" planning, including post-acquisition integration. Further, the planning firm was also more thorough in using the plans to develop and analyze its opportunities.

TABLE 3-2

CHANGES IN THE FREQUENCY OF PLANNING OVER TIME

	Degree of Planning			
	No Planning	"When-to" Planning	"How-to" Planning	Both types of Planning
Acquisition Programs before 1960	19	2	8	13
Acquisition Programs after 1960	17	2	6	21

As an example of the strong relationship between planning and thoroughness of execution, Table 3-3 presents data on the method for finding candidates. We divided the firms into three categories: (1) "passive" searchers, representing 29% of the firms, which waited until other firms approached them; (2) "broadcast" searchers (35%) which announced their requirements to

TABLE 3-3

"WHEN-TO" PLANNING AND THE ASSOCIATED SEARCH METHOD

	Search Method			
	Passive	Broadcast	Directed	Total
Firm did "when-to" Planning	6%	15%	25%	46%
Firm did not do "when-to" Planning	23%	20%	11%	54%
Total	29%	35%	36%	100%

management circles and appropriate brokers; and (3) "directed" searchers (36%) which not only defined their criteria in advance but also actively identified and pursued attractive candidates. The behavior demonstrated by the typical firms in these categories is described at greater length by Ansoff.[1] Table 3-3 shows the percentage of firms in each search category that did "when-to" planning and those that did not. A significantly greater proportion of firms (40% to 46%) who did "when-to" planning also engaged in active search (broadcast or directed) and thorough search methods, compared to nonplanners (only 31% of 54% used deliberate search). (Using the chi-square distribution, the probability is less than 0.001 that the perceived relationship is simply sample error.)

The Search for Acquisition Opportunities. As Table 3-3 shows, 36% of the acquiring firms engaged in intensive search for acquisition candidates, 35% used a planned but less focused broadcast method and 29% were passive recipients of suggestions, with no preconceived limitations on the candidates.

Table 3-4 shows the relative frequency of candidate sources for the acquiring firms in terms of the absolute number of candidates uncovered. This table used a three-point scale (three points for the most important source to a firm, fewer points for respectively less important sources for that firm).

[1] H. Igor Ansoff, *Corporate Strategy* (New York: McGraw-Hill, 1965), pp. 207 ff.

TABLE 3-4

SOURCE OF ACQUISITION CANDIDATES

Source	Points
Outside agencies	55
Inquiries from other firms	47
Broadcasting of interest to pertinent parties	45
Special staff analysis within firm	41
Contacting and visiting business associates	21

Although the table shows the most common source for all candidates to be some agency outside of the acquiring firm, relatively few of these candidates were actually acquired. Of the candidates whose acquisition was consummated, 69% of the initial contacts were made by the acquiring firm.

Responsibility for the search activity was usually assigned to an officer at the vice-presidential level or above, as shown by Table 3-5. A surprisingly small percentage of firms assigned the responsibility to a director of a special

TABLE 3-5

POSITION HOLDING PRIMARY RESPONSIBILITY FOR SEARCH ACTIVITY

Position	Percent of Firms
Board Chairman	11%
President	33%
Vice-President	44%
Staff Director	12%

staff function. Individual questionnaires reveal that the staff director was used almost exclusively in large firms which were acquiring a number of smaller firms—typically pursuing a conglomerate acquisition strategy.

Table 3-6 shows that only 5% of the firms that did extensive search felt that they achieved all of their objectives, as compared to 17% for those that did not use significant resources on the search process. However, as the objective measures of success will later show, the difference is probably due to the fact that the latter group had not explicitly formulated their objectives in advance of the search and, hence, had no real basis for comparison.

TABLE 3-6

PERCENTAGE OF SAMPLED FIRMS CATEGORIZED BY THE EXTENT
OF SEARCH EFFORT AND PERCEIVED OBJECTIVES ACHIEVED

| | Perceived Objectives Achieved[1] | | | |
	All	Most	Few	Total
Extensive Search[1]	5%	25%	9%	39%[2]
Passive Search	17%	32%	12%	61%
Total	22%	57%	21%	100%

1. Includes broadcast and directed types. Small differences from Table 3-3 are due to rounding off error.

2. In the last chapter, various characteristics of acquisition behavior, such as the extent of search will be related to more objective measures of success than self-report, ex post facto feelings of accomplishment. In this chapter, success is measured by management's perceptions of achievement as reported on the questionnaire response. The extent of search was not strongly related to the achievement of objectives for the acquisition program in terms of the accomplishments perceived by top management.

The Evaluation of Acquisition Candidates.   Only 14% of the firms who responded to the questionnaire had a formal budget assigned to the search and evaluation phases of the acquisition activity. In the acquiring firm, the number of people with full-time responsibility for seeking and evaluating acquisition candidates ranged from zero to six. The average was just below one. The average number of people who had a part-time responsibility for acquisition activity was just above one, with a range from zero to ten.

On the average, a firm seeking acquisitions uncovered about 20 candidates worthy of consideration. The number of potential acquisitions which passed a preliminary screening process by a firm varied from 2 to 350. For every acquisition actually consummated, there was an average of about 1.5 prospects per firm that were subjected to thorough evaluation requiring over one man-month of effort, with a range from zero to fifteen evaluations. There was, on the average, almost one case of extensive negotiation without acquisition for every acquisition that took place. The typical length of time from the first recognition of a firm as a prospect until the completion of the acquisition was about ten months. This period of evaluation ranged from one month to five years.

To examine the relationship between effort spent on evaluation of candidates and success of acquisitions, the respondents were divided into two groups. The first group thoroughly evaluated those candidates which passed a preliminary screening, using at least one man-month of evaluation effort per candidate. The second group did only a cursory evaluation of its candidates.

A surprising result was that, of the 48% of the firms that did evaluate candidates thoroughly, fewer acquisitions were judged by their management as being completely successful, and just as many failed as for the firms which did only cursory evaluation. Further, the firms that evaluated candidates thoroughly encountered a greater percentage of problems in executing their acquisitions.

A possible explanation for this result is again offered by possible differences in behavioral bias between planners and nonplanners. Firms which did a thorough evaluation formed definite expectations and were disappointed. Nonplanners apparently were willing to take the results as they found them.

Table 3-7 shows the percentages of firms which claimed to have encountered different types of acquisition problems, differentiating them also by their degree of evaluation effort. The total percentage adds to more than 100% because some firms encountered more than one type of problem.

The effects of different evaluation practices on the success of acquisition programs is further discussed in the last section of this chapter.

TABLE 3-7

CANDIDATE EVALUATION EFFORT AND OCCURRENCE OF
ACQUISITION PROBLEMS

Problem Type	Degree of Evaluation Effort	
	Thorough	Cursory
Personnel	57%	43%
Marketing	78%	22%
Integration	56%	44%
Synergy	63%	37%

The Integration of Acquisitions. A separate executive or management group was given primary responsibility for the majority of the post-acquisition integration activities in 53% of the acquisition programs. This responsibility was assigned to the board or its chairman in 24% of the cases, 8% to the president, 61% to a vice-president, and 15% to a special staff position. Firms were asked in the questionnaire whether or not they experienced integration problems. Table 3-8 relates these problems to the level of the person responsible for integration.

TABLE 3-8

THE OCCURRENCE OF INTEGRATION PROBLEMS AND
ORGANIZATIONAL LEVEL OF INTEGRATION RESPONSIBILITY

	Level of Responsibility			
	President	Vice-President	Staff Director	Total
Integration Problems Occurred	7%	29%	5%	41%
No Integration Problems Occurred	17%	32%	10%	59%
Total	24%	61%	15%	100%

As this table shows, when the assignment was made to the president or to a special staff director, a smaller proportion of firms experienced integration problems. However, only a small subsample of 36 firms provided data for this analysis.

In 35% of the sampled firms, little or no responsibility was assigned to the acquired firm. Another 35% assigned responsibility that was proportional to the relative sizes of the two firms, while the remaining 30% gave equal voice about integration matters to the acquired firm. Table 3-9 indicates that in those instances where the acquired firm had no voice in integration decisions, 42% of the acquisitions experienced integration problems (11/26). When the acquired firm had some voice but generally less than the acquiring firm, about 37% had integration problems (13/37). When the acquired firm had equal voice, the proportion of acquisitions experiencing integration problems dropped to 28% (11/39).

About 41% of the acquired firms were allowed to operate in a completely autonomous fashion; another 24% installed uniform policies and procedures

TABLE 3-9

PERCENTAGE OF INTEGRATION PROBLEM OCCURRENCE AND
INTEGRATION-DECISION PARTICIPATION BY ACQUIREE

	Responsibility in Integration Decisions			
	Equal	Proportional to firm size	None	Total
Integration Problems Occurred	11%	13%	11%	35%
No Integration Problems Occurred	28%	22%	15%	65%
Total	39%	35%	26%	100%

in the acquiring and the acquired firms; 16% of the acquisitions resulted in the integration of the functional areas only, while another 15% integrated all activities. Table 3-10 shows the percentage of responding firms, for each acquisition type, that completely integrated their acquisitions into their operations, those that only partially integrated, and those that operated their acquisitions autonomously.

TABLE 3-10

DEGREE OF INTEGRATION BY ACQUISITION TYPE

| Acquisition Type | Degree of Integration | | | |
	Complete Integration	Partial Integration	Autonomous Operation	Total
Horizontal	10%	11%	12%	33%
Vertical	4%	4%	5%	13%
Concentric	10%	7%	18%	35%
Conglomerate	2%	4%	13%	19%
Total	26%	26%	48%	100%

As would be expected, conglomerate firms practice the least degree of integration, and horizontal and vertical mergers, the most.

Since conglomerate acquisitions usually were not highly integrated into the operations of the acquiring firm, there were few integration problems among the conglomerates. Table 3-11 shows the percentage of acquiring firms who incurred integration problems for each of the acquisition strategy types.

TABLE 3-11

OCCURRENCE OF INTEGRATION PROBLEMS BY
ACQUISITION STRATEGY TYPE

Acquisition Type	Percentage Incurring Integration Problems
Horizontal	18%
Vertical	18%
Concentric	30%
Conglomerate	6%

In 34% of the acquisitions, integration activities took less than six months; for 18%, they lasted between six months and a year. About 23% of the acquisitions were integrated in a period greater than one year but less than two years, while 25% of the acquisitions took more than two years to integrate. The relationships between length of time to integrate and the occurrence of integration problems were also investigated. The proportion of acquisitions for which integration problems occurred was almost constant regardless of the time span of the integration activity.

Synergy. When seeking acquisition possibilities, 76% of the responding firms sought a "common thread" or "synergy," i.e., a close relation between skills and resources of the two firms. Table 3-12 shows the relative importance of different types of synergy, using a three-point scale.

TABLE 3-12

RELATIVE IMPORTANCE OF SYNERGY TYPES

Type of Synergy Sought	Points
Common sales administration, warehousing or distribution channels	61
Common technology and R & D	57
Common raw materials or products	50
Common types of top-management competencies	40
Common types of facilities or personnel skills	35

Of those firms that sought synergy in their acquisitions, about 30% derived synergistic benefits which exceeded management expectations, and 35% estimated benefits to be lower than expectations. Table 3-13 shows a relation between degree of integration of the acquired firm into the parent firm and the attainment of synergy. The proportion of acquisitions that attained synergy with autonomous operation was 58%; the proportion attaining synergy with complete integration was 76%.

TABLE 3-13

DEGREE OF INTEGRATION AND THE ATTAINMENT OF
SYNERGISTIC BENEFITS

Degree of Integration	Percent of Firms Attaining Synergy
Complete Integration	76
Partial Integration	62
No Integration	58

There is some evidence of a relationship between "how-to" planning and the attainment of synergy. As Table 3-14 shows, 64% (37/58) of those acquiring firms who sought synergy and who did "how-to" planning did, in fact, achieve synergy. About 57% (24/42) of those who did not do "how-to" planning achieved synergy. About 34% of the responding firms tried to attain more than one type of synergy in their acquisitions.

TABLE 3-14

"HOW-TO" PLANNING AND SYNERGY ATTAINMENT

	Existence of "How-To" Planning	
	Did Plan	Did Not Plan
Did Attain Synergy	37%	24%
Did Not Attain Synergy	21%	18%

Technological synergy was the most difficult to achieve with only 44% of the firms accomplishing their expectations for benefits from this synergy (12/27). According to Table 3-15, marketing synergy was accomplished by 60% of the firms that sought it (24/40) and the other types of synergy (predominantly managerial competencies) were attained by 67% of the firms that sought them.

TABLE 3-15

SYNERGY TYPE AND SYNERGY ATTAINMENT

	Synergy Attainment		
	Attained	Not Attained	Total
Marketing Synergy	24%	16%	40%
Technological Synergy Sought	12%	15%	27%
Other Synergies Sought	22%	11%	33%
Total	58%	42%	100%

Correlates of Acquisition Success and Failure. The major objectives of the acquisitions were all accomplished in the opinion of top management for about 21% of the responding firms. Partial success (most objectives satisfied) was attained in 59% of the acquisitions. About 20% were considered outright failures with few or no objectives met.

In 18% of the acquisitions, an unanticipated integration problem occurred. About 43% of the acquisitions resulted in personnel problems; synergy did not materialize in 11%; and market potentials were not achieved in 36% of the firms' reported legal problems, but this is the cause for not responding to the questionnaire, according to letters received from some firms.

More than 75% of the acquiring firms made forecasts of post-acquisition performance of the acquired firm prior to merging. In these cases, 40% of the acquisitions resulted in greater sales volume than was expected. However, 34% had lower sales than were forecast, and 26% had actual sales that approximately equalled the forecast.

Actual profit margins were more disappointing than sales when compared to forecasts. Almost 49% of the acquisitions had profit margins that were significantly less than forecasts. Only 26% had more favorable profit margins than were predicted. The disappointing profit margins were offset slightly by the better-than-expected sales so that the absolute level of profits was lower in only 45% of the acquisitions, higher in 34%, and about the same in 21%. These results are summarized in Table 3-16.

TABLE 3-16

RESULTS COMPARED TO FORECASTS

| | Actual Performance Measures | | | |
	Greater than Forecasts	About Equal to Forecasts	Less than Forecasts	Total
Sales	40%	26%	34%	100%
Earnings	34%	21%	45%	100%

In general, one might expect that those firms that thoroughly planned their acquisition programs and carefully executed their candidate search, evaluation, and integration activities would have a significantly greater incidence of successful acquisitions. The last chapter will show this to be the case when objective financial measures of performance are used to define success. In the present chapter, where the measures of success are the

TABLE 3-17

EXISTENCE OF PLANNING AND PERCEIVED OBJECTIVE ACHIEVEMENT

| | Perceived Objectives Obtained | | | |
	All	Most	Few	Total
No Planning	10%	18%	11%	39%
"When-to" Planning Only	2%	3%	2%	7%
"How-to" Planning Only	4%	12%	2%	18%
Both Types of Planning	9%	22%	5%	36%
Total	25%	55%	20%	100%

opinions of top managements regarding their acquisition accomplishments, there is little evidence to suggest that careful planning and executing of the acquisition program actually enhances the changes of success.

Table 3-17 shows the relationships between planning and the reported accomplishment of objectives.

Furthermore, those firms that submitted their acquisition candidates to a thorough evaluation achieved less reported accomplishment than firms that did a cursory evaluation. This is indicated in the data of Table 3-18.

TABLE 3-18

DEGREE OF CANDIDATE EVALUATION AND
PERCEIVED OBJECTIVE ACHIEVEMENT

	Perceived Objectives Obtained		
	All	Most	Few
Thorough Evaluation	7%	31%	10%
Cursory Evaluation	16%	26%	10%

Two reasons may account for this apparent failure of planning, when measured by subjective evaluation. First, the firms that did not plan had no explicit statement of expectations and hence, could more readily adjust their aspirations *ex post facto*. Second, a number of firms achieved success without careful planning and analysis because their acquisitions were relatively small firms whose operations were already well known to them. This occurred in the case of several vertical acquisitions where small customers or suppliers were acquired.

When the primary responsibility for the acquisition activities was assigned to the president of the acquiring firm, 88% of the acquisitions were reported to have accomplished all or most of their objectives. When the chairman of the board was assigned the responsibility, this percentage was 82%; with the vice-president, 78%; and with a staff director, 64%.

With the possible exception of the vertical acquisition strategy, the degree of success did not differ markedly for the different types of acquisitions. Table 3-19 shows the percentages of acquisitions reportedly achieving all, most, or few objectives, by acquisition type.

The relation between degree of integration and perceived success of the acquisition is not clear. As Table 3-20 shows, each degree of integration— from complete to autonomous operation—shows about the same distribution. Only when these data are broken into acquisition types does there appear to

TABLE 3-19

ACQUISITION TYPE AND THE PERCEIVED ACHIEVEMENT OF OBJECTIVES

| | Perceived Objectives Achieved | | |
Acquisition Type	All	Most	Few
Horizontal	6%	22%	8%
Vertical	4%	2%	1%
Concentric	8%	25%	6%
Conglomerate	2%	11%	5%

TABLE 3-20

DEGREE OF INTEGRATION AND PERCEIVED OBJECTIVES ACHIEVED

| | Perceived Objectives Achieved | | |
Degree of Integration	All	Most	Few
Complete	7%	17%	3%
Partial	7%	14%	5%
Autonomous Operation	11%	24%	12%

be an association, and then the sample size gets small (particularly for vertical acquisitions). Table 3-21 shows that horizontal acquisitions were slightly more successful when operated autonomously. There was no definite relation between success and degree of integration for vertical conglomerate acquisitions.

One of the most conclusive relationships discovered in this study is the correlation of the attainment of synergy with the perceived accomplishment

TABLE 3-21

DEGREE OF INTEGRATION AND PERCEIVED ACHIEVEMENT
OF OBJECTIVES BY ACQUISITION TYPE

Horizontal

| | Perceived Objectives Achieved | | |
Degree of Integration	All	Most	Few
Autonomous Operation	2%	6%	4%
Partial Integration	3%	7%	1%
Complete Integration	3%	7%	1%

Vertical

	Perceived Objectives Achieved		
Degree of Integration	All	Most	Few
Autonomous Integration	1%	3%	1%
Partial Integration	3%	0%	1%
Complete Integration	3%	2%	0%

Concentric

	Perceived Objectives Achieved		
Degree of Integration .	All	Most	Few
Autonomous Integration	6%	10%	3%
Partial Integration	0%	5%	2%
Complete Integration	1%	7%	1%

Conglomerate

	Perceived Objectives Achieved		
Degree of Integration	All	Most	Few
Autonomous Operation	2%	5%	4%
Partial Integration	1%	2%	1%
Complete Integration	0%	1%	1%

of the acquisition objectives. Table 3-22 shows that virtually all firms which attained synergy were successful (48/50), while roughly 60% among firms which attempted to seek synergy but failed considered themselves successful (18/28); similar views were held by firms that did not originally seek a synergistic effect in their acquisitions (13/22).

TABLE 3-22

SYNERGY ATTAINMENT AND THE PERCEIVED ACHIEVEMENT OF OBJECTIVES

	Perceived Objectives Achieved			
	All	Most	Few	Total
Synergy Not Sought	4%	9%	9%	22%
Synergy Not Attained	1%	17%	10%	28%
Synergy Attained	17%	31%	2%	50%
Total	22%	57%	21%	100%

Financial Vehicles for Acquisition. More than 57% of the acquired firms were purchased for cash, 24% were purchased entirely by an exchange of common stock, and 16% by a mixture of common stock and cash. The expected future profitability of the acquisition or its contribution to the profitability of the parent firm was the most important determinant of the price of the acquired firm. Table 3-23 shows the relative importance of several determinants of the price, using a two-point scale.

TABLE 3-23

RELATIVE IMPORTANCE OF PRICE DETERMINANTS

Determinant	Points
Expected future profitability	95
Market value	55
Outside appraisal	21
Other	14

Learning from Acquisitions. As a result of acquisition experience, 38% of the sampled firms have changed or intend to change their acquisition planning process in a significant manner, while 15% adopted minor changes. Of the firms that are changing their acquisition process, 43% are altering the objectives for acquisition; 44% are reassigning responsibility for the search and evaluation process; 51% are changing the staffing; and 40% will seek different characteristics of desirable acquisition candidates.

Consistent Acquisition Behavior. By far the most significant relationship that was identified in a statistical analysis of the questionnaire responses was the correlation among good planning and decision-making practices. These practices were:

1. Entrepreneurial type of action trigger—existence of strategic planning
2. Existence of preplanning effort
3. Directed search for candidates aimed at specific industries or types of technology
4. Extensive search—as compared to local search
5. Evaluation of a large number of alternatives
6. Thorough evaluation of all promising candidates
7. Existence of "when-to" planning
8. Existence of "how-to" planning

In performing the analysis, the investigators were seeking correlations between planning, searching, evaluation, and integration practices. Specifically, answers were being sought for such questions as: Is directed search activity usually found in firms who also evaluate a large number of acquisition candidates before making their decisions?

From the analysis, we discovered a dichotomy of practices. *The acquisition processes of the firms in the sample either exhibited all of the above practices or very few of them.* Characteristics of each of the firms common to both the questionnaire and the computer studies were examined in detail. Twenty-two firms indicated in their responses that they had used all eight of the planning/decision-making activities in their acquisition process. In most cases the remaining firms lacked four or more of the above characteristics.

Of the twenty-two firms with extensive planning, twenty were also firms on which objective performance data were available also. Forty of the 71 nonplanners had analogous data available. The subsample of twenty firms, when compared to the forty nonplanners, exhibited markedly different patterns of success in terms of the financial measures provided by the computer study. The results of the combined questionnaire-computer study will be covered in detail in Chapter 5.

Summary

The most important result of the quesionnaire study was the discovery that the respondents, with very few exceptions, either used planning and decision-making practices throughout the acquisition process or consistently did a very cursory analysis. This dichotomy allowed comparison of different aspects of acquisition behavior on the basis of objective performance measures. The dramatic results of this comparison are presented in Chapter 5.

Several interesting insights can be gleaned from the questionnaire responses. The action of those firms that initiated acquisition programs during the last decade did not differ much from the firms that started programs during the previous decade. However, most firms do change their acquisition procedures significantly as a result of the initial acquisitions.

The strength or weaknesses of current markets or marketing abilities of the firm provided the primary reasons for acquiring.

Those firms that did extensive planning in advance of acquiring reported about the same degree of success as those that did little planning, although these results are contradicted when objective, financial measures of success are used. As with planning activities, the firms that did extensive search and thorough evaluation of candidates fared no better than those that did not, in terms of their own perceptions of accomplishment. The most successful method of search in terms of the highest percentage of candidates eventually acquired were studies and inquiries by the acquiring firm.

There was no definite relationship between the degree of integration of the acquisition with the parent and the perceived success of the integration. However, when the acquired firm was allowed approximately equal participation in integration decisions, a smaller incidence of integration problems was reported.

One of the most conclusive findings of the questionnaire study was the relationship between synergy and success. While those firms that attained synergy in the acquisitions enjoyed a higher percentage of reported success than those that did not attain it, accomplishing synergy appears to be an elusive goal. Neither care in planning nor integration for synergistic effects was related to attainment. Managerial and marketing synergies were considerably easier to attain than technological synergy.

CHAPTER 4

PERFORMANCE MEASURES OF ACQUISITION ACTIVITY

SECTION 1: MODEL FOR ANALYSIS OF ACQUISITION PERFORMANCE

The computer analysis phase of the study is based on data supplied by Standard and Poor Compustat tape which contains sixty bits of data on financial performance of more than 900 firms for the period 1946-65. All relevant financial data are included. We elected to concern ourselves only with firms classified as manufacturing, whose Standard Industrial Classification number was between 2000 and 3999.

The selected sample was divided into acquiring and nonacquiring firms. Any firm which had at least one acquisition during the 1946-65 period and had an "acceptable" acquisition program was considered an acquiring firm. In brief, an acceptable program has an acquisition-free subperiod; it is described below in greater detail. The history of acquisitions, firm by firm, was obtained from Moody's *Handbook of Industrials* for the years 1946-65. A total of 395 firms were found to have acquisitions in this period. Of these, 271 had an acceptable acquisition program. Table 4-1 shows the distribution by number of acquisitions *within* the acquisition program. Note the preponderance of firms with programs containing only one or two acquisitions—66.0%.

Table 4-1 gives the distribution of the number of acquisitions by a firm which falls within the firm's acceptable acquisition program. This restriction and its implications are further explained under discussion of the "acceptable" acquisition program. We later explicitly tested the effects of the number of acquisitions on our results by altering the minimum number of acquisitions constituting an acceptable program.

An "Acceptable" Acquisition Program. A number of attributes of a firm are increased every time an acquisition is made: total sales, total assets, number of employees, all of which are directly related to increased size. The effects of acquisition on other important attributes such as growth rate, efficiency in use of capital, reaction of the stock market, are not clear. In

TABLE 4-1

DISTRIBUTION OF THE NUMBER OF ACQUISITIONS
IN EACH ACQUIRER'S PROGRAM

Number of Acquisitions	Number of Firms	Percentage of Total Firms
1	137	46.4
2	58	19.6
3	28	9.5
4	20	6.8
5	11	3.7
6	10	3.4
7	7	2.4
8	4	1.4
9	3	1.0
≥ 10	17	5.8
	295	100%

order to measure such effects, we defined an "acceptable" acquisition program to contain acquisition-free periods both before and after a series of acquisitions. By comparing performances during these respective periods, we were able to determine the effect of acquisitions on the nonobvious attributes and gain an understanding of the change in the dynamics of the firm.

We further required that not more than one year elapse between two successive acquisitions *during* the acquisition subperiod.

The minimum acceptable pre-acquisition period was four years; the minimum post-acquisition period, two years. We should have liked to use a longer post-acquisition period, but increasing the period would have drastically reduced the size of the acceptable sample, since there were very few firms which had at least three consecutive years of no acquisitions following an acceptable acquisition period.

A typical "acceptable" program might be as shown below, the X's representing years in which at least one acquisition took place:

```
year  1  2  3  4  5  6  7  8  9  10  11  12  13  14  15  16
...   0  0  0  0  0  X  X  0  X   X   X   0   X   0   0   X ....
      |        |                              |         |
         pre-              acquisition program    post-
         acquisition                              acquisition
         period                                   period
```

In this example we would be comparing the growth rate of the performance variables in years 14 and 15 (post-acquisition period) to those of years 1-5 (pre-acquisition period).

Limitations of Approach. Our approach suffers from two limitations. First, the short post-acquisition period allows for considerable bias caused by uncontrollable short-term influences on firm's performance which would tend to be washed out or minimized if we were able to make the post-acquisition period longer. Also, a two-year post-acquisition period may not allow enough time for complete integration of the acquired firms within the total corporate framework.

The second limitation of our approach is that requirement of "acceptable" programs eliminates many strongly acquisition-oriented firms, or at best, focuses attention on a fraction of their history. Firms such as Teledyne, Litton, Textron, etc., are not included in our sample, since they had no two-year periods of dormancy following a series of acquisitions.

The Measurement of Performance. In expectation that firms exhibiting differing rates of growth exhibit different acquisition patterns and results, for most of our study we stratified the acceptable sample on the basis of pre-acquisition sales growth. (As excursions, we also stratified by earnings and earnings/share and by the number of acquisitions. These results will be discussed in Section 4.) The sample was divided into three growth classes: low, medium, and high. Table 4-2 summarizes the results.

TABLE 4-2

SAMPLE SIZES IN EACH GROWTH CLASS

Group	Acquiring Firms	Nonacquiring[1] Firms	All Firms[1] on Tape
Low ≤4% growth	74	9	63
Medium 4% < X ≤ 10%	98	18	170
High > 10% growth	99	36	461
Total	271	63	694

1. Since these two samples have no defined post- and pre-acquisition periods, their growth class was determined by their average growth over the first ten years of this study. This also accounts for the apparent inconsistency of the numbers, summed horizontally, for the low-growth firms.

Table 4-3 shows the distribution of our acquiring firms by industry and by growth class. The numbers to the left of the industry name refer to the first two digits of that industry's SIC code.

TABLE 4-3

FIRMS IN GROWTH CATEGORIES: BREAKDOWN BY INDUSTRY

INDUSTRY	LOW GROWTH	MEDIUM GROWTH	HIGH GROWTH	TOTAL
20 Food Processing	18	19	7	44
21 Tobacco	4	2	1	7
22 Textiles	4	2	1	7
23 Clothing	1	3		4
24 Lumber				
25 Furniture	1	3		4
26 Paper		6	3	9
27 Printing	1	2	1	4
28 Chemicals	7	18	9	34
29 Petroleum Refining	4	9	6	19
30 Rubber	2	2	2	6
31 Leather	2	1		3
32 Stone, Glass, Clay	1	5	8	14
33 Primary Metals	5	10	5	20
34 Fabricated Metal Products	7	5	5	17
35 Machinery	17	7	15	39
36 Electrical Machinery	3	2	15	20
37 Transportation Equipment	13	7	13	33
38 Instruments, Clocks, Photographic	4	2	1	7
39 Miscellaneous Manufacturing	2	1	1	4
Totals	96	106	93	295[1]

NOTE: Sales growth during pre-acquisition period—firms with acceptable merger programs only.
1. Includes 24-firms later eliminated because of incomplete data record.

Performance Measures Used. The study encompasses twenty-one different measures of performance on thirteen separate variables. For most
variables, performance was measured in more than one way to minimize the
effects of biases of any one type of measure. Table 4-4 shows the
performance variables used and the type of measure used for each variable.

Two types of growth measures were used because each in itself has
weaknesses which may tend to bias or distort the data. The Type I measure
used is the mean of the yearly growth rates within the period. A firm with
greatly fluctuating performance would tend to have its performance biased
upward using this measure. A simple numerical illustration will demonstrate

TABLE 4-4

VARIABLES CALCULATED IN STUDY

Variable	Type Measure		
	I	II	III
Sales	X	X	
Earnings	X	X	
Earnings/Share	X	X	
Total Assets	X	X	
Earnings/Equity	X	X	
Dividends/Share		X	
Stock Price (Adjusted)		X	
Debt/Equity		X	X
Common Equity		X	X
Earnings/Total Equity		X	X
Price/Earnings Ratio (Adjusted)			X
Payout (Dividends/Earnings)			X
Price/Equity Ratio			X
TOTAL	5	10	6

Type Measures

I. Average of annual percentage growth

$$\frac{100}{N} \sum_{t=1}^{N} \frac{X_t - X_{t-1}}{X_{t-1}}$$

Where N = number of years in period and X_t = value of variable in t^{th} year of period.

II. Average percentage change over period

$$\frac{100}{N} \frac{X_N - X_1}{X_1}$$

III. Average value over period

$$\frac{1}{N} \sum_{t=1}^{N} X_t$$

the bias. Suppose the earnings/share of a firm are $1.00, $.10, and $.50 for these successive years. Then the growth in E/S would be

$$\frac{.10 - 1.00}{1.00} \ (100)\% = -90\% \quad \text{for year 2 and}$$

$$\frac{.50 - .10}{.10} \ (100)\% = 400\% \quad \text{for year 3, with an average annual}$$

growth of $\dfrac{(-90 + 400)}{2} = 155\%$

when, in reality, over the two years, earnings/share have managed to decline at an average rate of 25% per year.

The Type II measure of growth used is the more commonly used measure of growth that is obtained by subtracting the performance in the first year of the period from that of the last year, and dividing by the first-year value times the number of years in the period. This method of computing growth is not without its weaknesses, either. For example, if either the first- or last-year performance is not inordinately different from the surrounding years' performance, the growth rate will be distorted. Second, even if the firm experiences a steady growth in performance, the Type II, or usual growth calculation, will overstate the actual yearly percentage growth.

Comparison of the types of growth measures for any given growth variable allowed us to spot distortion caused by extreme conditions.

The third type of measure used is the simple average value of a variable over the measurement period. This type of measure is most amenable to such performance variables as price/earnings and debt/equity ratios, etc.

The Performance Variables. It is useful to give a brief description of exactly how each variable is measured, since there are alternative ways for measuring many of them.

1. *Sales:* Net sales as defined in standard accounting practices.
2. *Earnings:* Income after all operating and nonoperating income but before extraordinary income as listed in company's reports.
3. *Number of Shares Outstanding:* The number of shares represents the net number of common shares outstanding at the *year end,* excluding treasury shares and script. It makes no allowance for possible dilution through warrants, convertibles, or options, but does include stock dividends.
4. *Total Assets:* Current assets plus net plant plus other noncurrent assets (including net intangible assets and deferred items).
5. *Common Equity:* Common equity consists of surplus and surplus reserves, unamortized debt premium, deferred income taxes, and capital stock premium, less common treasury stock, intangible, unamortized debt discounts, capital stock expenses, accumulated unpaid preferred dividends, and the excess of involuntary liquidating value of outstanding preferred stock over carrying value.
6. *Dividends:* Dividends include only payment in cash or securities other than common stock.
7. *Total Capital:* Simple sum of noncurrent portion of long-term debt, common equity as defined above, and the number of preferred shares outstanding times the involuntary liquidating value per share.

8. *Stock Price:* This is the mean of the high and low price for the year divided by the share adjustment factor. This adjustment factor adjusts the current stock price for all splits and stock dividends. Hence, all year's prices are expressed in terms of an equivalent number of shares outstanding.

9. *Debt/Equity Ratio:* This is the ratio of all debt, both current and long term, to the net equity of the firm.

10. *Price/Earnings Ratio:* This is normal price/earnings ratio adjusted for the relative change in the price/earnings ratio for the Dow Jones Industrial Index at the year end, using 1947 as the base year.

Restrictions Placed on Performance Variables in the Computer Program. These restrictions are two in nature: one, in computing or smoothing the growth ratio; and two, in setting an upper bound on any particular growth variable.

In an effort to negate the effects of great fluctuations in our data (usually the earnings and sales data, since all other data tend not to fluctuate violently), the computer program includes a check of the yearly sales and earnings data with smoothing functions to adjust violent fluctuations. If the data is fluctuating to such a degree as to make smoothing unreasonable, the program rejects this firm from the sample.

This procedure significantly lessens the bias experienced in applying our Type I growth-rate measure, since fluctuations of large proportions are either smoothed or the firm is rejected from the sample.

The second check involves placing an upper bound of 100% per year as the limiting growth rate on all Type II growth variables. Since our statistical significance test (to be described in detail) involves a simple summation of all individual growth rates, an extraordinarily high individual growth rate for a particular firm could significantly bias our results, even in a sample as large as the one we use: hence, the need to place an upper bound on growth. In practice, this restriction affected less than 2% of our sample. The use of this upper bound tends to minimize the faults of our Type II measure, and together with the other smoothing process, tends to bring the Type I and Type II measures into a closer relationship.

The Computer Program. Appendix B is a sample print-out of our program. Note that the sample is split into growth classes, with the pre-acquisition, post-acquisition, the difference between the pre- and post-, and the total 20-year-period growth rates printed across the page for each variable. Additionally, the one or zero just to the right of the difference column signifies whether the difference is significant at the .05 level, using a one-way analysis of variance test. Column Five gives the value of the test statistic (± 1.645 represents significance at the .05 level). Columns Six through Eight give the average value for the variable being tested during the first year of the study, the last year before the acquisition program is begun, and the last year of the study, respectively.

The program is designed to yield this same information for all individual firms by simply changing one card in the program. Additionally, it can easily be combined with the program for questionnaire analysis responses to yield correlation with any particular questionnaire variable.

The basic prorgram contains over 850 statements and takes approximately 2.5 minutes to execute. Appendix C gives explanations in the right margin of the purpose of each phase of the program.

SECTION 2: COMPARISON OF PERFORMANCE BY GROWTH CLASS

Analysis of Computer Study Results. In this section we will discuss in detail the comparison, both qualitatively and statistically, of pre- and post-acquisitions performance for the low-, the medium-, and the fast-growth firms, as defined in Section 1. The question of major interest to us is whether any of the growth categories derived special advantages from the acquisition activity.

Test of Significance Used. The statistical test used is the standard one-way analysis of variance test which can be found in any standard statistical text. This test assumes that the samples are from normal distributions with equal variances. The test hypothesis is that the means of the two samples are equal. Although this is the most widely used test of significance utilized in the type of sampling we were conducting, it has inherent weaknesses in the assumption of a normal distribution and equal variances. Fortunately, the Central Limit theorem helps to minimize the bias of the former assumption, but the assumption of equal variances must simply be lived with. A check of the standard deviations of the samples indicates that, in fact, even with the relatively large sample sizes with which we were dealing, the variances do not appear to be anywhere near equal.

Nonparametric testing was used in all analyses of the combination of the computer and questionnaire studies, specifically the Wilcoxon two-sample signed rank test, and the H-test. Both of these methods make no simplifying assumptions as to normality or equal variances.

Post- vs. Pre-Acquisition Performance. Tables 4-5 and 4-6 give a summary (by growth class), of the effects of acquisition programs on performance.

TABLE 4-5

SUMMARY OF POST-ACQUISITION VERSUS PRE-ACQUISITION PERFORMANCE FOR ALL PERFORMANCE MEASURES TESTED

	LOW-GROWTH FIRMS			MEDIUM-GROWTH FIRMS			HIGH-GROWTH FIRMS			TOTAL SAMPLE		
	Pre-Acq.	Post-Acq.	% Diff.	Pre-Acq.	Post-Acq.	% Diff.	Pre-Acq.	Post-Acq.	% Diff.	Pre-Acq.	Post-Acq.*	% Diff.
Sales Growth I	.88	6.90	684%	4.94	6.98	41.3%	12.10	6.95	-42.6%	6.45	6.95	7.8%
Earnings Growth I	3.78	24.57	550%	7.02	10.89	55.1%	15.79	11.56	-26.8%	9.34	14.87	59.2%
Earnings/Share Growth I	3.54	23.84	673%	6.49	10.03	54.5%	14.11	10.39	-26.4%	8.47	13.93	64.5%
Total Assets Growth I	2.80	4.91	75.4%	5.52	6.71	21.6%	11.35	7.52	-33.7%	6.91	6.52	-5.6%
Earnings/Common Equity Growth I	-.80	19.09	*	.14	3.49	2393%	3.83	2.87	-25.1%	1.23	7.53	512%
Sales Growth II	-.16	7.71	*	6.83	7.31	7.0%	26.72	7.93	-70.3%	12.18	7.65	-37.2%
Earnings Growth II	-4.52	21.81	*	4.40	8.43	91.6%	24.49	10.99	-55.1%	9.36	13.02	39.1%
Earnings/Share Growth II	-4.51	20.30	*	3.63	7.53	107.4%	19.83	9.49	-52.1%	7.32	11.73	60.2%
Total Assets Growth II	3.97	5.54	39.5%	8.52	7.25	-14.9%	24.32	8.66	-64.4%	13.05	7.30	44.1%
Earnings/Common Equity Growth II	-7.93	16.77	*	-3.25	.63	*	2.22	.03	98.6%	-2.53	4.82	*
Payout Ratio Growth II	10.55	2.88	-72.7%	6.10	.95	-84.4%	5.54	3.38	-39.0%	7.11	2.37	-66.7%
Total Equity Growth II	5.67	4.89	-13.8%	9.60	6.88	-28.3%	20.64	8.72	-27.8%	12.56	7.01	-44.2%
Earnings/Total Capital Growth II	-7.50	14.62	*	-2.39	1.40	*	2.96	.60	-79.7%	-1.83	4.72	*
Adjusted Stock Price Growth II	3.92	13.33	240%	12.77	13.71	7.4%	32.57	12.68	-61.1%	17.59	13.23	24.8%
Total Debt/Equity Growth II	-2.84	3.39	*	.07	1.33	1800%	10.81	.07	-99.4%	3.20	1.43	-55.3%
Price/Earnings Ratio III	8.61	7.68	-10.8%	7.35	7.90	7.5%	8.20	9.33	13.8%	8.01	8.36	0.0%
Debt/Equity Ratio III	.47	.52	10.6%	.48	.46	-4.2%	.68	.66	-2.9%	.55	.55	0.0%
Payout Ratio III	.60	.52	-13.3%	.47	.52	10.6%	.44	.54	22.7%	.49	.53	8.2%
Price/Equity Ratio III	.61	.99	62.3%	.62	1.10	77.4%	.59	1.52	157.6%	.61	1.22	100.0%
Total Equity III	96.98	139.15	43.5%	114.40	185.26	61.9%	137.54	278.82	102.7%	118.10	206.85	75.1%
Earnings/Total Assets III	.10	.08	-20.0%	.12	.09	-25.0%	.14	.10	-28.6%	.12	.09	-25.0%
Earnings/Share	1.79	1.75	-2.0%	1.83	2.13	16.0%	1.57	2.00	27.0%	1.72	1.98	15.0%
Stock Price	16.89	22.38	32.4%	16.45	26.91	63.0%	13.26	29.84	125.0%	15.40	26.74	74.0%
Number in Sample		74.00			98.00			99.00			271.00	

*Cannot be calculated

55

TABLE 4-6

VALUE OF TEST STATISTIC AND CONFIDENCE LEVEL
FOR EACH VARIABLE BY GROWTH CLASS

Variable	LOW GROWTH		MEDIUM GROWTH		HIGH GROWTH		TOTAL SAMPLE	
Sales Growth I	5.77	(.01)	2.96	(.01)	-5.32	(.01)	.85	(.20)
Earnings Growth I	3.68	(.01)	1.76	(.04)	-1.43	(.08)	2.59	(.01)
Earnings/Share Growth I	3.64	(.01)	1.63	(.05)	-1.26	(.10)	2.60	(.01)
Total Assets Growth II	2.46	(.01)	1.86	(.03)	-4.57	(.01)	-.83	(.20)
Earnings/Common Equity Growth I	3.67	(.01)	1.76	(.04)	-.37	(.35)	3.22	(.01)
Sales Growth II	6.49	(.01)	.67	(.25)	-7.90	(.01)	-3.85	(.01)
Earnings Growth II	4.59	(.01)	2.33	(.01)	-2.77	(.01)	1.40	(.08)
Earnings/Share Growth II	4.56	(.01)	2.32	(.01)	-2.29	(.01)	1.80	(.04)
Total Assets Growth II	1.80	(.04)	-1.68	(.05)	-7.42	(.01)	-5.93	(.01)
Earnings/Common Equity Growth II	4.37	(.01)	2.89	(.01)	-.84	(.20)	3.68	(.01)
Payout Ratio Growth II	-1.98	(.03)	-2.53	(.01)	-.75	(.23)	-2.84	(.01)
Total Equity Growth II	-.91	(.18)	-3.78	(.01)	-6.04	(.01)	-6.50	(.01)
Earnings/Total Capital Growth II	4.51	(.01)	2.62	(.01)	-.89	(.18)	3.57	(.01)
Stock Price Growth II	2.77	(.01)	.40	(.34)	-4.52	(.01)	-2.95	(.01)
Debt/Equity Growth II	3.23	(.01)	.82	(.20)	-4.45	(.01)	-1.42	(.08)
Price/Earnings Ratio	-1.95	(.03)	1.10	(.14)	2.50	(.01)	-1.27	(.10)
Debt/Equity Ratio	1.36	(.09)	-.56	(.29)	-.68	(.24)	.12	(.45)
Payout Ratio	-2.04	(.02)	2.24	(.01)	4.40	(.01)	1.99	(.02)
Price/Equity Ratio	5.08	(.01)	6.63	(.01)	7.33	(.01)	10.45	(.01)
Total Equity	2.67	(.02)	4.89	(.01)	3.63	(.01)	5.56	(.01)
Earnings/Total Equity	-4.03	(.01)	-5.67	(.01)	-8.10	(.01)	-10.36	(.01)

Test statistic (confidence level)
± 1.65 indicates significance at .05 level

Table 4-5 shows the pre- and post-acquisition percentage change in the performance as well as growth rates for Type I and Type II measures and the percentage change in the mean value of performance variables for Type III measures. This is shown for each growth class and for the total sample. Table 4-6 gives a statistical interpretation of these same results. The main figure in each cell represents the value of the test statistic and the figure in parentheses is the association level of significance (±1.645 is the .05 level of significance). Figures 4-1 and 4-3 are plots of the results of nine selected *growth rates* from Table 4-5 by growth class. Figures 4-4 and 4-5 present eight *average*

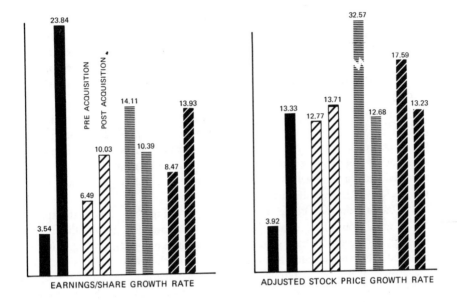

EARNINGS/SHARE GROWTH RATE

ADJUSTED STOCK PRICE GROWTH RATE

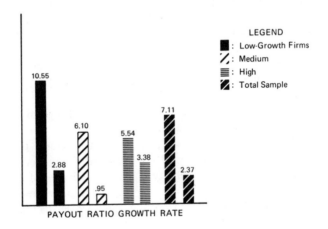

PAYOUT RATIO GROWTH RATE

LEGEND

■ : Low-Growth Firms
▧ : Medium
☰ : High
▨ : Total Sample

Fig. 4-1.
Comparison of Pre- and Post-Acquisition
Growth Rates (by Growth Class).

performance levels before and after acquisition. Measures included in Figure 4-1—earnings per share, dividend payout, and the market value of the stock—are of special interest to the stockholder since they measure his current income from the firm and the market value of his investment in the firm. For the 271 firms included in our study, the differential effects of acquisition activity are:

1. Firms initially experiencing little (less than 4% per year) internal sales growth show dramatic increases in the *rates of growth* of the stockholder variables. Low-growth firms increased their earnings per share growth rate by a factor of almost seven times. On the other hand, medium-growth firms averaged only a 55% gain and high-growth firms actually performed worse than before their acquisition activity.

2. As seen in the middle row of bar charts in Figure 4-2, the marketplace did a good job of recognizing the effects of acquisitions on the firm's earnings. However, for each growth class, the change in the growth rate in the adjusted stock price failed to match that of the change in earnings. For the low-growth firms, $G:E/S$ (growth rate in earnings/share) increased 673%, while $G:SP$ (growth rate in stock price) increased only 240%. Hence, the low-growth firm's price/earnings ratio failed to grow at a corresponding rate to $G:E/S$, and in fact, in this sample, the average price/earnings ratio growth rate declined by 10.8%. Thus the marketplace either failed to alter its expectations of the future growth of low-growth firms sufficiently fast to maintain the original price/earnings level, or it reviewed this dramatic change in earnings growth as only a transient event and not indicative of the firms' real expected growth rate.

For the medium-growth firms also, the change in $G:SP$ (6.7%), failed to keep pace with the improvement in $G:E/S$ (55%).

The high-growth firms again performed poorly. $G:E/S$ for high-growth firms averages declined by 27%, while $G:SP$ plummeted by 61%.

3. The acquisition activity substantially depressed the growth of dividend payout ratio. As Figure 4-1 and Table 4-5 show, low- and medium-growth (73% and 84% decrease) firms did much worse than high-growth ones (39% decrease).

Size Variables (Magnitude of Operations). Sales volume, total assets, and total equity all automatically increase in size as a result of acquisitions. Figure 4-2 shows that their respective growth rates before and after acquisitions do not necessarily follow suit.

1. The change in growth rates of sales and total assets resembles very closely those of earnings/share and stock price. Little need be added in the

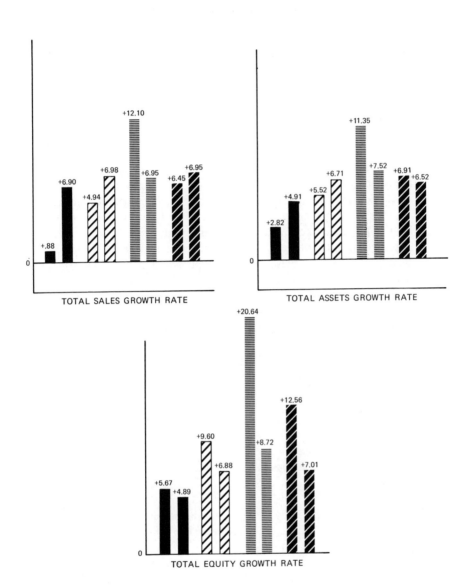

Fig. 4-2.
Comparison of Pre- and Post-Acquisition
Growth Rates (by Growth Class).

way of analysis here, only that again high-growth firms experience an *actual* decrease in their sales growth rate due to acquisition activity. This implies that fast growers generally acquire firms that are slow growers.

2. For each growth class, rate growth of total equity slows down as a result of the acquisition program. The effect is most pronounced for high-growth firms, less for medium and least for slow growers (-58%, -28%, -14%, respectively).

Efficiency of Capital Variables. Earnings/common equity, earnings/total assets, and debt/equity ratio are significant measures of the firm's efficiency.

1. Probably of most importance is the ability (or inability) of the firm to improve its over-all efficiency in the use of all types of capital. As shown in Figure 4-3, both the low- and medium-growth firms demonstrated greatly improved growth of returns on total capital. Whereas, prior to their acquisition programs, these firms had experienced an actual decay in $G:E/TA$ (growth in earnings on total assets was -7.50% and -2.39% for low- and medium-growth firms respectively), their post-acquisition operations were improved to such a point as to reverse this process of decay and actually increase their respective $G:E/TAs$ to 14.62% and 1.40%.

For the high-growth firms, the now familiar pattern was maintained, that of a reduced growth rate in efficiency of assets (2.96% to .60%).

2. Figure 4-3 shows that relative debt/equity ratio growth increased very significantly in slow-growth firms and medium-growth firms and declined equally significantly in high-growth firms. However, the absolute growth rates in the former two cases remained modest.

Mean Performance Variables. The performance attributes shown in Figures 4-1 to 4-3 use Class I and Class II measures of the growth rates before and after acquisition. The over-all impression from these figures is that firms which were growing slowly at the outset very successfully enhanced their growth rate on practically every significant performance ratio. Fast-growing firms, on the other hand, seem to have taken a penalty all along the line in terms of reduced growth rates.

A different picture emerges when we turn from growth rates to measures of the firm's average position during the pre- and post-acquisition periods. This is demonstrated in Figures 4-4 and 4-5.

1. The average price/earnings ratio of the slow-growth firms dropped by 10.8% during the post-acquisition period. The actual stock price did rise by 32%; however, earnings per share declined 2%, producing a net drop in price/earnings.

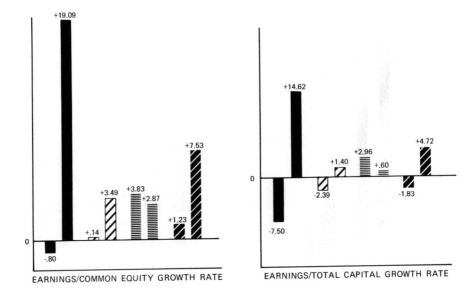

EARNINGS/COMMON EQUITY GROWTH RATE

EARNINGS/TOTAL CAPITAL GROWTH RATE

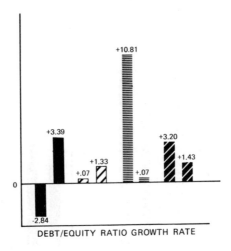

DEBT/EQUITY RATIO GROWTH RATE

Fig. 4-3.
Comparison of Pre- and Post-Acquisition
Growth Rates (by Growth Class).

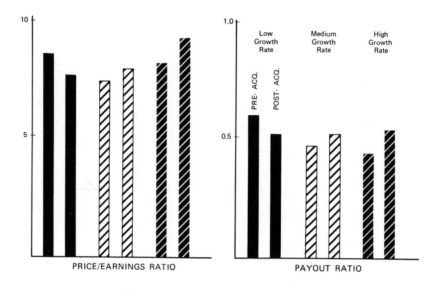

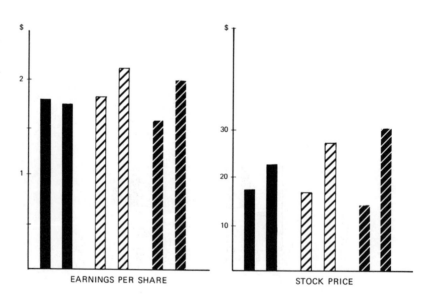

Fig. 4-4.
Comparison of Pre- and Post-Acquisition
Mean Performance Values (by Growth Class).

62

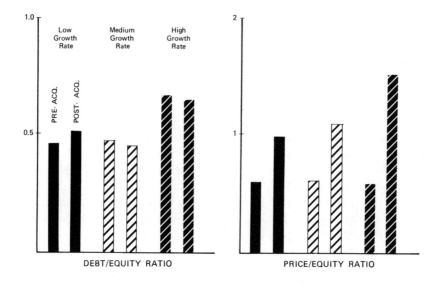

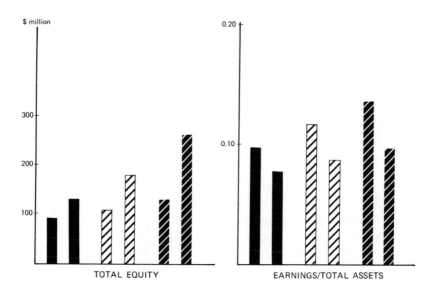

Fig. 4-5.
Comparison of Pre- and Post-Acquisition
Mean Performance Values (by Growth Class).

2. By contrast, fast-growth firms experienced a fourfold greater increase in price, a 27% increase in earnings, and a consequent 13% increase in the price/earnings ratio.

3. Middle-growth firms scored positively on all counts but not as impressively as fast-growth firms: 63% gain in price, 16% gain in earnings/share, and an 8% gain in price/earnings.

4. Fast-growing firms were equally impressive performers in improving price per dollar of equity with a 157% gain (see Figure 4-5). But both slow and medium firms also better than doubled their price/equity ratios. On the whole, the market appears to reward aggressive activity by appreciating the value of invested capital.

5. As could be predicted, the average value of the equity increased in all cases, but again the fast-growth firms scored better than twice the gain (103%) of the slow-growth firms (43%).

6. On the other hand, earnings on total assets declined about equally and substantially (20%, 25%, and 29%) across the board with high-growth firms being the greatest losers of efficiency. This result may be due to the shortness of our post-acquisition period and the consequent presence of a "post-acquisition integration period" observed in acquisitions.

7. Behavior of debt/equity ratios was consistent with their growth rates. Low-growth firms increased their relative indebtedness substantially (11%) while medium- and high-growth firms decreased it slightly (4% and 3% respectively).

8. Dividend payout was cut sharply for slow-growth firms (13%) consistently with previously discussed growth rates. It was increased moderately by medium-growth firms (11%) and, surprisingly, substantially increased (23%) by high-growth firms.

Summary

Comparison of changes in the growth characteristics of acquirers shows that low-growth firms gained spectacularly for a number of significant variables, whereas high-growth acquirers suffered actual declines in growth of such variables as earnings/share, sales, stock price, etc. The opposite effect occurs with respect to the relative changes in the mean level of performance between pre- and post-acquisition periods. The low-growth firms took penalties in their price/earnings, payout, debt/equity ratios, and in earnings/share, while the medium- and high-growth acquirers were able to increase their levels of performance in all of these categories.

Thus it appears that there was a trade-off in the accomplishment: high-growth firms, which already had the growth image, suffered a loss in growth characteristics but improved their average position; low-growth firms were able to increase their growth characteristics but only at the expense of the position variables. The market did not respond to the low-growth firms, producing a decrease in their price/earnings ratio, while rewarding the "growers" with an increase.

SECTION 3: THE COMPARISON OF ACQUIRING TO NONACQUIRING FIRMS

How might we have expected the acquiring firms to perform had they not sought external answers to growth? Since the over-all period of our study, 1946-65, was one of general economic prosperity, it is possible that apparent improvements from acquisitions were merely the product of economic progress. To gain insight into this possibility, we compared, by growth class, the performances of our sample firms with comparable nonacquiring firms from the same industry.

To permit comparison of performance of the acquiring and nonacquiring firms during similar calendar periods, we selected an early period in the study, 1947-52, and a later period, 1960-65, as periods comparable to the pre- and post-acquisition periods, respectively, for the acquiring firms. These periods were selected to match as closely as possible with the mean pre- and post-acquisition periods of the acquiring firms. By designing the period of study in this manner, we are able to test the hypothesis that mergers are beneficial by simply comparing the relative changes in performances of the two samples from the pre- to post-acquisition periods.

The sample of nonacquirers was composed of all manufacturing firms on the Compustat tape which had a complete 20-year history of data, and of course, which had no acquisitions during the period 1947-65. As with the "acquire" sample, these firms were grouped into growth classes by their sales growth for the pseudo period 1947-52: 0-4% for low-growth firms, 4-10% for medium-growth firms, and greater than 10% for the high-growth firms. Because the period 1947-52 is an artificially constructed selection period, tests were run varying the length of this selection period to determine whether it significantly altered the compositions of our sample classes. The end result was a conclusion that the distribution of nonacquirers among growth classes was extremely insensitive to the length of the selection period.

A total of 82 nonacquiring firms were used (as compared to our acquirers sample of 271)—low-growth firms, medium growers, and high-growth firms. Their "pre-acquisition" financial characteristics are shown on Tables 4-11 through 4-14. The one possibly significant difference between the samples of acquiring firms and nonacquiring firms is that the acquiring sample tended to have a larger average equity base in the pre-acquisition period. This is easily seen by noting the comparative average total equity figures for both samples on the Tables 4-11 through 4-14.

Comparability of an acquiring group of firms with a nonacquiring one, however, implies one or both of the following assumptions:

1. Percentage growth rates are not functions of the size of the firms in the sample; and/or
2. The mean size for the two samples in each growth class is the same.

A later section in this chapter on stratification analysis supports the first assumption.

There is also a possibility of a bias in favor of nonacquirers caused by the particular selection of the later period, 1960-65, for the nonacquiring firms. This is due to the fact that the 1960-65 period was one of greater change in prosperity relative to almost any random post-acquisition period that may be chosen over the time span of 1955-65.

Data Tables. Tables 4-7 through 4-14 and Figures 4-6 through 4-9 summarize the results of our analysis. In Tables 4-7 to 4-10, the data (for what we felt were the most important performance measures) are broken out by period. Each cell of these tables contains the ratio of mean value of the performance measure of the acquiring firms to that of the nonmerging sample, given by growth class. Because of negative values of some of the measures, some cells have only the actual value for both samples (for instance, in Row 1, Column 1 of Table 4-7, the growth ratio in sales of the acquiring and nonacquiring firms is -.16% and 1.32%, respectively).

Tables 4-11 through 4-14 give a complete listing of the data for every performance measure calculated, again organized by growth class. However, for almost all relevant analysis, Tables 4-7 to 4-10 should suffice.

To summarize the entire 19-year pattern on relative growth between acquirers and nonacquirers, the yearly growth patterns for earnings/share, sales, stock price, and earnings on total assets for the two samples are plotted against each other (by growth class) in Figures 4-6 through 4-9.

Analysis of Results. We will first discuss results of comparing acquirers and nonacquirers for the pre- and post-acquisition periods and then draw inferences about the over-all performance of acquirers and nonacquirers.

I. Pre-Acquisition Period

Pre-acquisition behavior can be expected to yield clues to the reasons why or how firms are motivated to seek acquisitions. Two general answers are possible:

1. Acquiring firms were poor performers relative to others in their growth class or to their industry and thus were spurred into action by the desire to improve their performance.

2. That acquisition was internally triggered by aggressive management. Comparison of pre-acquisition performance of acquirers and non-acquirers provide several clues toward an answer.

   A. Total Sample. Analysis of the total sample presents a somewhat muddled picture. From Row 4, Table 4-7, acquiring firms as a whole had superior growth rates in such critical variables as earnings/share, earnings on total capital, and stock price. They lagged in sales, growth, and maintained an average, lower price/earnings and earnings/total capital ratios. Hence, it is not at all clear that the acquiring firms as a whole were motivated by poorer performance, although a mild case for such a point may be made by referring pointedly to sales growth and the price/earnings ratios. But, as the lower right-hand quadrants of Figures 4-6 through 4-8 demonstrate, in the years between 1947 and 1952, the general pre-acquisition years, there was little difference in the growth patterns of the acquiring and nonacquiring firms.

   B. Low and Medium Growth Firms. Table 4-7 shows that the low-growth acquirers initially grew more rapidly (or declined less rapidly) than their nonmerging counterparts on all growth yardsticks, except sales. However, the nonmerging firms enjoyed higher price/earnings, earnings/common equity, and earnings/total assets ratios.

   If, as suggested in the last section, the low-growth firms were seeking to improve their growth image, they had little external motivation to seek mergers. On the other hand, if we take the view that price/earnings ratio and sales growth tend to be dominant managerial performance criteria, their failure in comparison to similar companies becomes the apparent source of motivation to acquire. A third possible trigger to action was the declining growth rates on all significant variables. This suggests that management was motivated by its own past history and not by external indicators.

   Finally, and equally probably in our opinion, the trigger may have been a comparison of the firm's performance, not with similar low (or medium) growers, but the entire sample. A comparison of the first column in Tables 4-11 and 4-12 to Column 1 or 2 in Table 4-14 suggests a very strong external trigger toward acquisition. In summary, there is considerable evidence that acquisition activity for medium and slow growers was triggered by Reason One given above.

C. High-Growth Firms. Unlike the low- and medium-growth firms, the high-growth acquirers had no apparent performance motivator for seeking acquisitions. From Row 3, Table 4-7, and by comparing Columns 1 and 2 of Table 4-13, it is easily seen that, in almost all performance measures, the high-growth acquirers dominated all of their peer groups.

Thus we are left with either the very nebulous conclusion that the high-growth firms' managements simply wandered into favorable merger situations, or the much more likely conclusion that the managements of these high-growth acquirers are self-motivated, aggressive, and deliberately seeking opportunities for their firms without waiting for adverse results.

II. Post-Acquisition Period

The raw data for all firms for the post-acquisition period is given in Columns 3 and 4 of Tables 4-11 through 4-14 and is summarized in comparative ratio form in Table 4-8.

Low-growth firms are seen to be inferior performers on all criteria except earnings on total capital and earnings on equity. Where it is recalled from the preceding section that the efficiency in the use of capital actually declined as a result of acquisition, the two growth rates lose much of their significance.

The medium-growth firms are uniformly poor on growth ratios. The only positive advantage to the acquirers is a 30% higher price/equity position.

High-growth firms show some advantages to the acquirers in the price/earnings and price/equity variables. The entire sample is similarly mixed and appears to show no clear advantage to acquiring firms.

III. Comparison of Increments in Pre- to Post-Acquisition Performance

A further insight is provided by the *increments* in their respective performance from pre- to post-acquisition. This is shown in Table 4-9. The data in the table gives the *ratio* of the *percentage point* change in the performance measure for the acquiring sample to that for the nonacquirers of the same growth class. For example, from Table 4-11, we see that the change in sale growth for low-growth acquirers was 7.87

percentage points [7.71 - (-.16)] whereas the corresponding change for nonacquirers was 11.40 [12.72 - 1.32]. The resultant ratio of

$$\frac{7.87}{11.40} = .69$$

is given in Row 1, Column 1 of Table 4-9. Since we are dealing in percentage point changes, there is the danger of scale effects. However, this is in all but one case not a major factor, since the values of the performance variables for acquirers and nonacquirers are of the same order of magnitude.

A. Growth Rate Variables. For all growth classes, the change in all but three performance measures of acquirers is less than that for nonacquirers if the changes are negative. That is, if performance improved for both groups, nonacquirers improved more, and if performance decreased, nonacquirers' performance decreased less.

For example, looking at Row 4 of Table 4-9 (all firms), sales growth for acquirers decreased by 1.42 times that of the non-acquirers, whereas earnings per share growth increased by only .22 times that of the nonacquirers.

The lone bright spot for acquirers, at least in regard to growth-rate changes, is in the apparent improvement in efficiency of capital for low-growth firms. From Row 1, Columns 5 and 6 of Table 4-9, note that the changes in earnings on total capital and earnings on common equity growth rates for low-growth acquirers was over twice that for nonacquirers (2.10 and 2.32 respectively). Again, looking at the new data in Table 4-11, Rows 10 and 13 also corroborate this implication. But even the encouragement of this statistic is diminished when we compare medium- and high-growth firms: note Rows 2 and 3, Columns 5 and 6 of Table 4-9.

Hence, if growth is a primary management criterion of effectiveness, then there is little encouragement that we can impart to acquisition programs in general *as a means of growth.*

B. Average Value Ratios. The last three columns of Table 4-9 give the ratio of the changes in the mean value of three pertinent performance measures for acquirers and nonacquirers. The surprising implication indicated here (in view of the growth-rate discussion) is the dominance of performance of the acquiring firms.

In each growth class, the acquiring firms had a more favorable change in price/earnings and in price/equity ratios. This is directly opposite to what might have been expected in light of their growth performance. The natural question to be answered is why the marketplace apparently rewarded the acquirers with a higher price than was justified by their relative improvement in growth.

Two answers can be hypothesized.

One is that the market is, in fact, a reflection on anticipated future performance and that the post-acquisition period was not long enough to truly reflect the long-term benefits of the acquisition programs to the acquiring firms. Thus, the better performance which the market anticipated from acquiring firms had not yet materialized.

The other possible explanation is that the market reacts to the evidence of acquisition activity and does not evaluate the financial results in the manner performed in this study. Therefore, it rewards the activists with higher price/earnings and price/equity ratios.

IV. Total Period Analysis

Figures 4-6 through 4-9 reflect the effects on performance by acquisition over the entire period under study.

Looking at the total samples, plotted in the lower right-hand quadrants of Figures 4-6 through 4-8 (the graphs for E/S, sales, and stock price growth respectively), note that the nonacquirers performed consistently better than acquirers although not by a very large margin. On the basis of the total sample, one would conclude that mergers and acquisitions are not a preferred growth method. This holds true *even* for sales growth, which we would expect to be favorable to acquirers.

However, moving inside the growth classifications, we find a somewhat more differentiated picture. Specifically, low-growth acquirers, whose pre-acquisition performance closely paralleled that of their nonacquiring counterparts and in some cases dominated it, were completely dominated by the nonacquirers in the later years of the study, suggesting that external solutions to internal growth problems are transient at best with little long-run benefit.

Somewhat the same remarks hold for the medium-growth firms, only not so strongly.

The high-growth acquirers outstrip the nonacquirers both in sales and earnings per share. On the other hand, there was no significant difference in the growth of stock prices when we consider the entire 20-year history of data. This may be due to the fact that high-growth

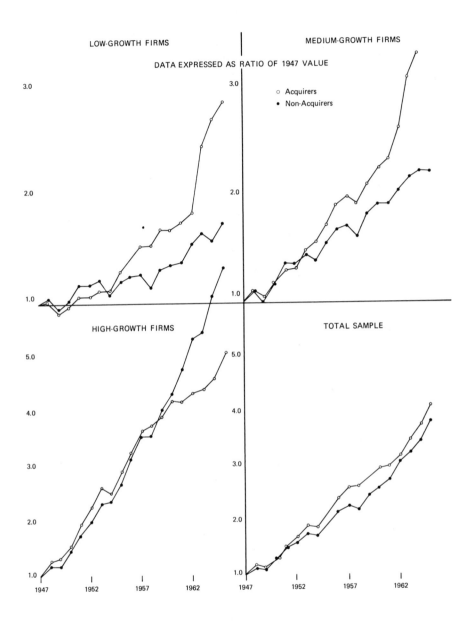

LOW-GROWTH FIRMS

MEDIUM-GROWTH FIRMS

DATA EXPRESSED AS RATIO OF 1947 VALUE

o Acquirers
• Non-Acquirers

HIGH-GROWTH FIRMS

TOTAL SAMPLE

1947   1952   1957   1962   1947   1952   1957   1962

Fig. 4-6.
Comparative Sales Growth
(by Growth Class).

71

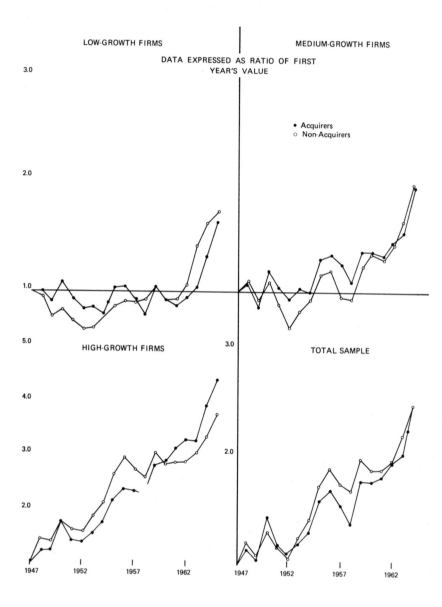

Fig. 4-7.
Comparative Earnings/Share Growth
(by Growth Class).

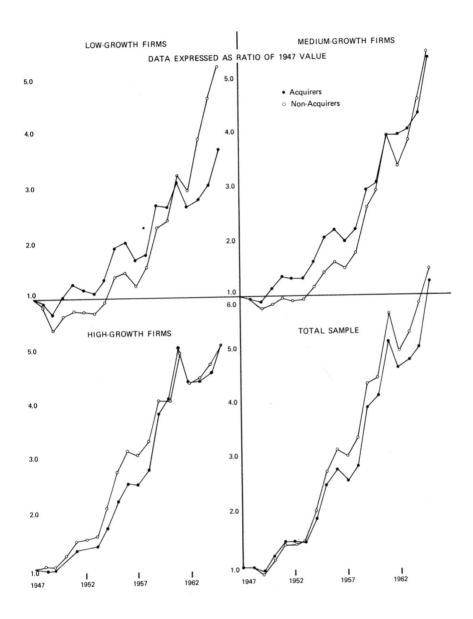

Fig. 4-8.
Comparative Stock Price Growth
(by Growth Class).

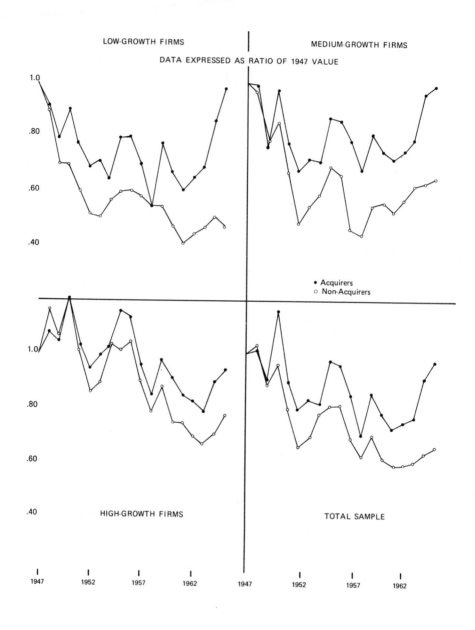

LOW-GROWTH FIRMS · MEDIUM-GROWTH FIRMS

DATA EXPRESSED AS RATIO OF 1947 VALUE

• Acquirers
○ Non-Acquirers

HIGH-GROWTH FIRMS · TOTAL SAMPLE

1947   1952   1957   1962   1947   1952   1957   1962

Fig. 4-9.
Comparative Earnings/Total Capital Growth

acquirers were active acquirers throughout the 20-year period. Thus, they continued acquiring after our "official" post-acquisition period. The long-run growth effects did not, therefore, become evident.

Finally, Figure 4-9 presents a very interesting picture of the relative efficiency in the use of assets by acquirers and nonacquirers. In all growth categories, acquirers made more effective use of their assets (as measured by return on assets) than nonacquirers. Here again we are left with an impression of the relative aggressiveness of the managements of the two types of firms. The acquiring firms' managements appear to have made better use of internal resources and of external financing than nonacquirers. This inference is supported by Table 4-14.

Summary
1. Pre-acquisition performance suggests that slow-growth firms embarked on acquisition as a result of an accumulated history of deteriorating performance, and/or as a result of inferior current performance relative to the total sample.
2. On the other hand, acquisitions made by high-growth firms appear to be the result of a restless management drive to continue improving the firm's performance.
3. On the basis of the 20-year history of the sample as a whole, one would conclude that acquisitions do not pay and, in fact, are an inferior method of growth.
4. When analyzed by growth category, this conclusion is strengthened for low-growth firms: the acquirers did much poorer than nonacquirers, both on the post- to pre-acquisition comparison and the total history.
5. On the other hand, while high-growth acquirers showed indifferent performance on pre- versus post-comparisons, they were distinctly superior to nonacquirers on both price/earnings and price/equity ratios when total history is considered.
6. The acquirers in all classes were clearly more skillful in stemming a downward trend in the return on total capital employed in the firm. This is due in part to use of higher debt leverage.

TABLE 4-7

PRE-ACQUISITION PERIOD

	LOW GROWTH	MEDIUM GROWTH	HIGH GROWTH	ALL FIRMS
RATIO OF GROWTH RATE OF MERGING FIRMS TO NONMERGING FIRMS				
Sales	-.16/1.32	.99	.98	.82
Earnings.	-4.32/-7.00	-4.40/-6.04	1.63	2.70
Earnings/Share	-4.51/-7.34	2.63/-6.09	1.53	3.00
Stock Price	3.42/-2.72	12.77/-2.91	1.38	1.94
Earnings/Total Capital	-7.50/-9.88	-2.39/-10.17	2.96/-1.67	-1.83/-6.16
Earnings/Common Equity	-7.93/-10.21	-3.25/-9.45	2.22/-.35	-2.53/-5.44
Total Debt/Equity	-2.84/-4.03	.020	.42	.27
RATIOS OF AVERAGE VALUES				
Price/Earnings	.83	.75	1.17	.93
Price/Equity	.74	1.01	2.36	1.22
Earnings/Total Capital	.56	.92	.78	.80

TABLE 4-8

POST-ACQUISITION PERIOD

	LOW GROWTH	MEDIUM GROWTH	HIGH GROWTH	ALL FIRMS
RATIO OF GROWTH RATE OF MERGING FIRMS TO NONMERGING FIRMS				
Sales	.61	.76	.64	.65
Earnings	.99	.32	.51	.56
Earnings/Share	.99	.28	.33	.53
Stock Price	.43	.43	.48	.45
Earnings/Total Capital	22.8	.19	1.27	2.00
Earnings/Common Equity	37.4	.11	.03/-.25	3.24
Total Debt Equity	.65	.71	.07/-.95	.98
RATIOS OF AVERAGE VALUES				
Price/Earnings	.90	1.03	1.21	1.05
Price/Equity	.91	1.31	1.28	1.74
Earnings/Total Capital	.57	.90	.71	.75

TABLE 4-9

COMPARATIVE CHANGES IN VARIABLES BETWEEN
PRE- AND POST- ACQUISITION PERIODS

	LOW GROWTH	MEDIUM GROWTH	HIGH GROWTH	ALL FIRMS
RATIO OF CHANGE IN GROWTH RATES				
Sales	.69	.18	(-) 1.26	(-) 1.42
Earnings	.97	.12	$\frac{-13.50}{+6.50}$	.19
Earnings/Share	.86	.12	$\frac{-10.34}{+7.68}$	.22
Stock Price	.28	.03	$\frac{-19.89}{+2.71}$	$\frac{-4.36}{(-) 22.52}$
Capital Total	2.10	.22	$\frac{-2.36}{+2.14}$	.77
Earnings/Common Equity	2.32	.26	$\frac{-2.19}{+.10}$	1.06
Total Debt/Equity	.67	.27	(-) .73	(-) .19
RATIOS OF AVERAGE VALUES				
Price/Earnings	(-).52	$\frac{.65}{-2.04}$	1.59	$\frac{+.35}{-.70}$
Price/Equity	1.28	2.09	.99	1.07
Earnings/Total Capital	(-) 1.00	(-)1.00	(-) 1.00	(-) 1.00

$\frac{\Delta \text{ MERGING FIRMS}}{\Delta \text{ NONMERGING FIRMS}}$

TABLE 4-10

TOTAL PERIOD, 1947-1965

	LOW GROWTH	MEDIUM GROWTH	HIGH GROWTH	ALL FIRMS
RATIO OF GROWTH RATE OF MERGING FIRMS TO NONMERGING FIRMS				
Sales	.55	.95	1.04	.85
Earnings	.95	1.04	.70	.67
Earnings/Share	.70	.86	.48	.48
Stock Price	.88	1.40	.36	.51
Earnings/Total Capital	-1.37/-2.75	-1.46/-1.63	-1.21/-.61	-1.34/-1.46
Earnings/Common Equity	-1.49/-2.68	-1.96/-1.70	-1.20/-.78	-1.55/-1.53
Total Debt/Equity	.58	.51	.84	.65
RATIOS OF AVERAGE VALUES				
Price/Earnings	.92	.90	1.17	1.00
Price/Equity	.75	1.02	1.11	.97
Earnings Total Capital	.69	1.00	.75	.78

TABLE 4-11

COMPARISON OF MERGING AND NONMERGING FIRMS
LOW-GROWTH FIRMS COMPARISON

	Pre-Acquisition		Post-Acquisition		Total Period	
	Acq.	Nonacq.	Acq.	Nonacq.	Acq.	Nonacq.
Sales Growth I	.88	2.45	6.90	8.02	5.44	6.62
Earnings Growth I	3.78	4.91	24.57	10.23	16.46	8.72
Earnings/Share Growth I	3.54	4.59	23.84	13.06	14.95	8.52
Total Assets Growth I	2.80	3.10	4.91	7.10	5.71	6.15
Earnings Common Equity Growth I	-.80	.77	19.09	4.21	9.47	2.94
Sales Growth II	-.16	1.32	7.71	12.72	5.50	9.87
Earnings Growth II	-4.52	-7.00	21.81	22.15	4.30	4.53
Earnings/Share Growth II	-4.51	-7.34	20.30	20.50	2.78	3.99
Total Assets Growth II	3.97	3.52	5.54	18.06	7.07	11.53
Earnings/Common Equity Growth II	-7.93	-10.21	16.77	.45	-1.49	-2.68
Payout Ratio Growth II	10.55	10.92	2.88	2.46	2.72	4.87
Total Equity Growth II	5.67	5.54	4.89	12.55	6.94	12.91
Earnings/Total Capital	-7.50	-9.88	14.62	.64	-1.37	-2.75
Adjusted Stock Price	3.92	-2.72	13.33	31.17	10.07	11.48
Total Debt/Equity Growth II	-2.84	-4.03	3.39	5.21	1.11	1.93
Price Earnings Ratio III	8.61	10.37	7.68	8.58	8.40	9.13
Debt/Equity Ratio	.47	.37	.52	.38	.49	.38
Payout Ratio	.60	.62	.52	.65	.57	.64
Price/Equity	.61	.82	.99	1.09	.76	1.01
Total Equity	96.98	21.74	139.15	36.78	116.29	32.21
Earnings/Total Assets	.10	.15	.08	.13	.09	.13
Stock Price	16.89	12.26	22.38	17.17	19.56	15.68
Earnings/Share	1.79	1.44	1.75	1.34	1.77	1.37

TABLE 4-12

COMPARISON OF MERGING AND NONMERGING FIRMS
MEDIUM-GROWTH FIRMS COMPARISON

	Pre-Acquisition		Post-Acquisition		Total Period	
	Acq.	Nonacq.	Acq.	Nonacq.	Acq.	Nonacq.
Sales Growth I	4.94	5.23	6.98	27.21	7.47	22.42
Earnings Growth I	7.02	-2.25	10.89	13.96	10.68	9.65
Earnings/Share Growth I	6.49	-2.27	10.03	13.65	9.37	9.42
Total Assets Growth I	5.52	4.65	6.71	7.39	7.67	6.95
Earnings Common Equity Growth I	.14	-7.73	3.49	6.80	1.94	2.73
Sales Growth II	6.83	6.94	7.31	9.61	9.35	10.52
Earnings Growth II	4.40	-6.04	8.43	26.50	6.82	6.54
Earnings/Share Growth II	3.63	-6.09	7.53	26.50	4.97	5.77
Total Assets Growth II	8.52	6.33	7.25	12.15	10.96	12.91
Earnings/Common Equity Growth II	-3.25	-9.45	.63	5.51	-1.96	-1.70
Payout Ratio Growth II	6.10	12.33	.95	-2.37	2.79	1.29
Total Equity Growth II	9.60	7.40	6.88	10.47	11.14	12.65
Earnings/Total Capital	-2.39	-10.17	1.40	7.32	-1.46	-1.63
Adjusted Stock Price	12.77	-2.91	13.71	31.49	21.82	15.54
Total Debt/Equity Growth II	.07	3.39	1.33	1.87	1.23	2.40
Price Earnings Ratio III	7.35	9.72	7.90	7.68	7.50	8.29
Debt/Equity Ratio	.48	.51	.46	.51	.47	.51
Payout Ratio	.47	.57	.52	.47	.49	.50
Price/Equity	.62	.61	1.10	.84	.79	.77
Total Equity	114.40	24.93	185.26	41.63	139.49	36.41
Earnings/Total Assets	.12	.13	.09	.10	.11	.11
Stock Price	16.45	10.64	26.91	17.30	20.51	15.24
Earnings/Share	1.83	1.23	2.13	1.49	1.93	1.41

TABLE 4-13

COMPARISON OF MERGING AND NONMERGING FIRMS
HIGH-GROWTH FIRMS COMPARISON

	Pre-Acquisition		Post-Acquisition		Total Period	
	Acq.	Nonacq.	Acq.	Nonacq.	Acq.	Nonacq.
Sales Growth I	12.10	15.64	6.95	8.16	13.21	11.34
Earnings Growth I	15.79	14.72	11.56	15.53	16.84	16.34
Earnings/Share Growth I	14.11	13.82	10.39	14.66	14.34	15.38
Total Assets Growth I	11.35	16.17	7.52	8.80	12.90	11.76
Earnings/Common Equity Growth I	3.83	2.50	2.87	4.16	3.70	4.11
Sales Growth II	26.72	27.22	7.93	12.34	26.67	25.60
Earnings Growth II	24.49	15.00	10.99	21.50	20.28	29.05
Earnings/Share Growth II	19.83	12.87	9.49	20.55	12.76	26.66
Total Assets Growth II	24.32	27.30	8.66	16.12	28.99	33.92
Earnings/Common Equity Growth II	2.22	-.35	.03	-.25	-1.20	-.78
Payout Ratio Growth II	5.54	5.83	3.38	2.97	4.20	2.12
Total Equity Growth II	20.64	18.62	8.72	19.33	25.61	34.60
Earnings/Total Capital	2.96	-1.67	.60	.47	-1.21	-.61
Adjusted Stock Price	32.57	101.60	12.68	26.37	39.02	107.88
Total Debt/Equity Growth II	10.81	25.64	.07	-.95	4.22	5.04
Price/Earnings Ratio III	8.20	6.97	9.33	7.68	8.73	7.47
Debt/Equity Ratio	.68	.59	.66	.64	.68	.63
Payout Ratio	.44	.40	.54	.40	.48	.40
Price/Equity Ratio	.59	.25	1.52	1.19	1.00	.90
Total Equity	137.54	94.87	278.82	224.86	201.02	184.36
Earnings/Total Assets	.14	.18	.10	.14	.12	.16
Stock Price	13.26	7.13	29.84	25.11	21.21	19.60
Earnings/Share	1.57	1.14	2.00	2.03	1.77	1.76

TABLE 4-14

COMPARISON OF MERGING AND NONMERGING FIRMS
ALL FIRMS

	Pre-Acquisition		Post-Acquisition		Total Period	
	Acq.	Nonacq.	Acq.	Nonacq.	Acq.	Nonacq.
Sales Growth I	6.45	9.31	6.95	13.23	9.01	13.05
Earnings Growth I	9.34	7.54	14.87	13.69	14.51	12.50
Earnings/Share Growth I	8.47	7.02	13.92	13.16	12.71	11.94
Total Assets Growth I	6.91	9.57	6.52	7.97	9.04	8.96
Earnings Common Equity Growth I	1.23	7.71	7.53	4.88	4.64	3.42
Sales Growth II	12.18	14.83	7.65	11.71	14.63	17.33
Earnings Growth II	9.36	3.45	13.02	23.01	11.05	16.43
Earnings/Share Growth II	7.32	2.36	11.73	22.13	7.22	14.97
Total Assets Growth II	13.05	15.29	7.30	14.24	16.48	22.27
Earnings/Common Equity Growth II	-2.53	-5.44	4.82	1.49	-1.55	-1.53
Payout Ratio Growth II	7.11	8.94	2.37	1.40	3.28	2.63
Total Equity Growth II	12.56	12.10	7.01	15.13	15.28	22.89
Earnings Total/Capital	-l.83	-6.16	4.72	2.35	-1.34	-1.46
Adjusted Stock Price	17.59	45.57	13.23	29.03	24.90	57.24
Total Debt/Equity Growth II	3.20	11.71	1.43	1.46	2.29	3.50
Price/Earnings III	8.01	8.62	8.36	7.92	8.19	8.14
Debt/Equity Ratio	.55	.51	:55	.54	.55	.53
Payout Ratio	.49	.51	.53	.49	.51	.49
Price/Equity Ratio	.61	.50	1.22	1.07	.86	.89
Total Equity	118.10	21.74	206.85	36.78	155.63	103.86
Earnings/Total Assets	.12	.15	.09	.12	.11	.14
Stock Price	15.40	9.45	26.74	20.89	20.51	17.38
Earnings/Share	1.72	1.24	1.98	1.70	1.83	1.56

SECTION 4: STRATIFICATION ANALYSIS

Separation of the total sample into growth classes yielded significant differences. In search of additional insights, we stratified our sample in four different ways: by sales growth, earnings growth, sales volume prior to the acquisition program, and by the number of acquisitions included in the program.

Since sales and earnings are normally highly correlated, one would expect very little difference in the performance of firms grouped according to these two variables, and indeed we found little. In general, earnings growth tends to be slower than sales growth for any one firm. Thus, using the same percentage growth rate of 4% or less as the cutoff limits for low class, we found more firms in the sales grouping than in the earnings grouping. However, the distinctive differences in performance over growth classes which was exhibited when the sample was split by sales growth remained very similar when the sample was sliced by earnings growth. The similarities of results are demonstrated in Figures 4-10 and 4-11.

Somewhat different results were obtained when the sample was stratified by actual sales volume in the last year preceding the acquisition program. This is illustrated in Figure 4-12. The small firms (sales below $30 million) performed in much the same manner as our low growth firms, showing remarkably strong progress in growth rates. So, in general, did medium-growth firms correspond well to medium-sized firms (sales between $30 million and $100 million). But our large firms (greater than $100 million in sales) performed distinctly better than the high sales growth firms. This is illustrated by a comparison of Figures 4-10 and 4-12.

When the sample is split according to the number of acquisitions made by the firm during the acquisition period, it appears that the degree of acquisition activity has no observable correlation with the perceived performance. This is somewhat surprising, since one might expect that the greater the number of acquisitions, the greater the change in performance, either positively or negatively. Figure 4-13 shows that this is not the case. No clear differences are observable in growth rate changes between active and inactive firms.

Table 4-15 presents an analysis of statistical significance of our results (at 5% confidence level). It can be seen that stratification by variables other than the number of acquisitions generally produces highly significant differences between post- and pre-acquisition results. On the other hand, stratification by number of acquisitions is generally insignificant.

Interpretation of Data, Table 4-15. The numbers in each of the cells of Table 4-15 represent the value of the test statistic used in each stratification method. As a general guide, the higher the absolute value of the number, the more significant the variable, with the underlined figures indicating significance at a 95% confidence level.

By comparing the values of the test statistic for each subclass, one can observe the ability of any stratification type of discriminate among acquisition effects.

For example, when stratified by pre-acquisition sales growth, performance improvement and acquisition activity are highly correlated; yet when stratified by the number of acquisitions, earnings per share and acquisition benefits are significantly correlated. In general, any statistic with an absolute value greater than 1.65 implies a significant effect, with the higher the absolute value, the greater the significance.

Summary

In our main study we stratified the total sample into three subclasses, according to sales growth. This has shown interesting differences in the behavior of firms which is not observable when the total sample is analyzed. Virtually identical results are obtained when the sample is stratified by pre-acquisition earnings growth.

Stratification of the sample by the number of acquisitions shows no significant differences in performance improvement between active and less active acquirers.

A very interesting conclusion is that the large firms (sales greater than $100 million) demonstrated better performance than our subclass of high-growth firms.

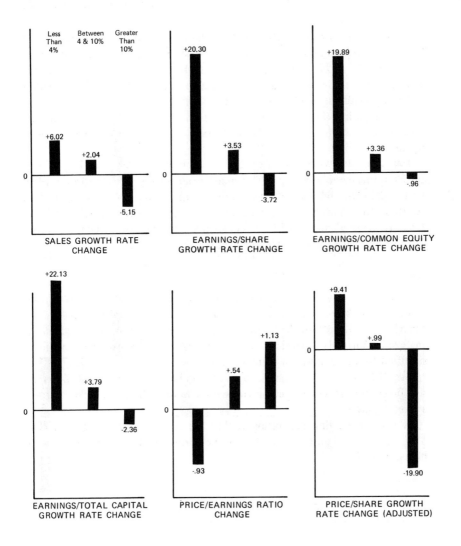

Fig. 4-10.
Pre- to Post-Acquisition Change in Performance
(Change Measured in Percentage Points).
Acquisition Sample Stratified by Sales Growth.

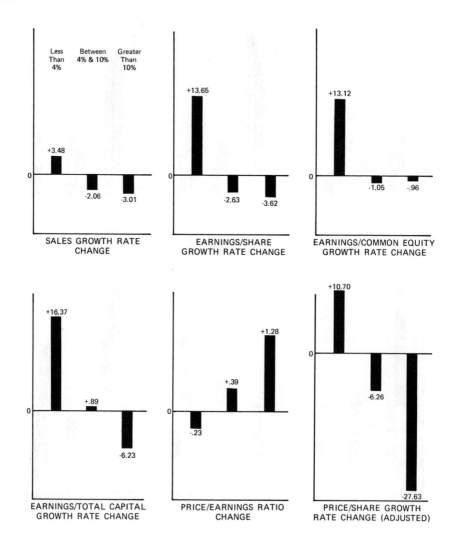

Fig. 4-11.
Pre- to Post-Acquisition Change in Performance
(Change Measured in Percentage Points).
Acquisition Sample Stratified by Earnings Growth.

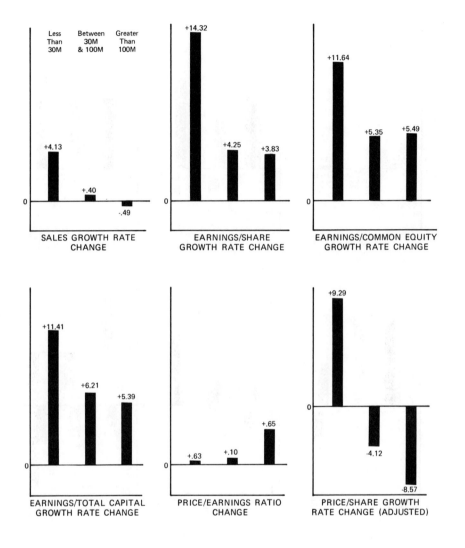

Fig. 4-12.
Pre- to Post-Acquisition Change in Performance
(Change Measured in Percentage Points).
Acquisition Sample Stratified by Sales Volume.

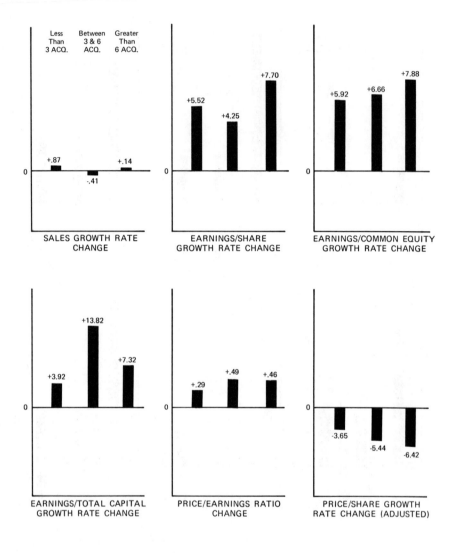

Fig. 4-13.
Pre- to Post-Acquisition Change in Performance
(Change Measured in Percentage Points).
Acquisition Sample Stratified by Number of Acquisitions.

TABLE 4-15

VARIANCE ANALYSIS OF STRATIFICATION METHODS

STRATIFICATION BY:

PERFORMANCE VARIABLE	Total Sample	SALES GROWTH			EARNINGS GROWTH			SALES VOLUME			NUMBER OF ACQUISITIONS		
		Low Growth	Medium Growth	High Growth	Low Growth	Medium Growth	High Growth	<30M	30-100M	>100M	1 - 2	3 - 6	>6
Sales Growth I	.85	5.77	1.96	-5.32	4.77	-1.32	-3.00	2.50	.40	-.64	1.31	-.29	.07
Earnings Growth I	2.59	3.68	1.76	-1.13	4.33	-.77	-1.40	2.77	1.05	1.54	2.44	.74	1.27
Earnings/Share Growth I	2.60	3.64	1.63	-1.26	4.18	-.83	-1.13	2.78	1.01	1.63	2.42	.73	1.38
Total Assets Growth I	-.83	2.46	1.86	-4.57	2.12	-.50	-3.44	1.58	-.54	-1.54	.54	-2.01	-.29
Earnings/Common Equity Growth I	3.22	3.67	1.76	-.37	4.20	-.41	-.33	2.53	1.31	2.69	2.83	1.19	1.65
Sales Growth II	-3.85	6.49	.67	-7.90	2.17	-3.04	-5.94	.96	-2.39	-4.10	-2.75	-2.31	-1.43
Earnings Growth II	1.40	4.59	2.33	-2.77	6.05	-.07	-4.01	1.46	.44	.74	.84	1.31	.09
Earnings/Share Growth II	1.80	4.56	2.32	-2.29	5.99	-.02	-3.48	1.66	.63	1.14	1.07	1.51	.35
Total Assets Growth II	-5.93	1.80	-1.68	-7.42	-.55	-3.35	-6.28	-.64	-3.63	-4.91	-4.55	-3.55	-2.02
Earnings/Common Equity Growth II	3.68	4.37	2.89	-.84	5.37	.80	-2.04	2.43	1.87	+2.95	2.84	2.27	1.01
Payout Ratio Growth II	-2.84	-1.98	-2.53	-.75	-2.84	.71	-.80	-1.49	-.68	-2.83	-1.46	-1.76	-4.78
Total Equity Growth II	-6.50	-.91	-3.78	-6.04	-2.54	-5.35	-5.48	-.78	-5.45	-5.68	-5.09	-3.45	-2.13
Earnings Total Capital Growth II	3.57	4.51	2.62	-.89	5.81	.35	-2.38	2.84	1.68	2.56	2.57	2.36	1.14
Employees Growth II	-2.95	1.26	-.90	-5.09	.04	-2.31	-3.17	-1.17	-.32	-3.24	-1.29	-2.49	-1.66
Stock Price Growth (Adjusted)	-2.00	2.77	.40	-4.52	4.43	-2.80	-6.32	1.67	-1.07	-3.02	-1.28	-1.34	-1.26
Total Debt/Equity Growth II	-1.42	3.23	.82	-4.45	1.31	-.63	-3.08	-.59	.02	-1.71	.25	-1.51	-1.78
Earnings/Employees Growth II	-2.39	1.14	-.55	-3.06	.72	-1.77	-4.15	-.90	-1.42	-1.72	-2.09	-1.12	-.73
Price/Earnings Ratio (Adjusted)	1.27	-1.95	1.10	2.50	-.55	.78	2.65	.06	.19	1.88	1.25	-.59	.36
Debt/Equity Ratio	.12	-1.36	-.56	-.68	1.53	-1.04	-.94	.66	1.20	-1.24	-1.12	.36	1.87
Payout Ratio III	1.99	-2.04	2.24	4.40	-1.01	2.66	3.92	-2.04	.83	3.25	2.17	.28	.96
Price/Equity Ratio	10.45	5.08	6.63	7.33	7.42	5.64	6.63	3.57	6.32	7.81	8.55	4.17	5.19
Total Equity	5.56	2.67	4.80	3.63	4.90	4.22	3.39	6.08	10.19	5.18	3.79	3.51	3.80
Earnings Total Assets	-10.36	-4.03	-5.67	-8.10	-7.29	-5.21	-5.58	-2.81	-7.26	-7.24	-7.76	-5.95	-3.72
Number in Sample	271	74	98	99	140	44	87	38	104	129	180	62	29

Group Breakdown:	Low	Medium	High
Sales & Earnings Growth	0 - 4%	4 - 10%	> 10%
Sales Volume	0 - 30M	30 - 100M	> 100M
Number of Acquisitions	1 - 2	3 - 6	> 6

Chapter 5

PLANNING AND ACQUISITION PERFORMANCE

SECTION 1: ACQUISITION BEHAVIOR AND FINANCIAL PERFORMANCE

Table 5-1 is a summary of the statistical tests run between each performance variable used in the Compustat study and each characteristic of managerial behavior explored in the questionnaire. The general statistical tests applied were the Wilcoxon Signed Rank and H Tests as given in any standard statistical text. Along the top of the table is listed each questionnaire characteristic with each possible response having a separate column. The characteristics are described in Chapter 3 or are response alternatives from the questionnaire (e.g., the Degree of Integration is taken from Question 24, Part I). The financial performance variables are listed vertically. Thus each cell in the table contains a statistical comparison of the particular performance variable related to that cell to the corresponding questionnaire characteristic.

For example, the upper left cell compares the type of action trigger employed and the change in the sales growth rate of the firm. The upper figures within the block represent the median value of the sales growth rate change for firms which indicated, respectively, entrepreneurial, planner, or reactor types of action trigger. In our example, firms having an entrepreneurial type of action trigger (e.g., strategic planning) experience a median growth rate change in sales of 2.94 percentage points, whereas planner firms had a median -4.26 percentage points change, and reactors, a 1.33 change.

The entire table contains some 483 (21 x 23) one-to-one statistical analyses. Rather than examine all 483 tests, we shall focus on only a handful of the more significant results, which are arranged by the type of questionnaire variable type.

TABLE 5-1

THE RELATIONSHIP OF MANAGERIAL BEHAVIOR AND PERFORMANCE VARIABLES

Variable Number	Compustat Variable		Action Trigger Type			Action Trigger Type		Type of Search		
	Questionnaire Variable →		Enterpre-neurial	Planning	Reactor	Preplanning	No Preplanning	Passive	Broadcast	Directed
1	Sales Growth Rate Change	I	2.94	-4.26	1.33	1.15	-5.03	-2.38	-3.02	3.66
2	Earnings Growth Rate Change	I	22.46	.50	8.07	8.73	.61	2.27	.61	17.55
3	Earnings/Shared Growth Rate Change	I	21.23	.67	8.07	8.91	.58	.67	1.54	21.23
4	Total Assets Growth Rate Change	I	.07	-2.31	-.09	-1.11	-1.15	.62	-2.08	-.09
5	Earnings/Common Equity Growth Rate Change	I	13.58	3.09	9.42	8.94	3.09	8.09	3.09	14.41
6	Sales Growth Rate Change	II	2.69	-6.01	1.48	1.70	-8.07	-3.74	-3.63	2.69
7	Earnings Growth Rate Change	II	20.89	3.46	8.07	9.52	1.30	1.30	3.97	14.88
8	Earnings/Share Growth Rate Change	II	19.92	3.17	9.33	9.89	3.70	3.17	3.70	15.06
9	Total Assets Growth Rate Change	II	-.03	-7.34	.07	-1.72	-1.90	1.35	-2.73	-.26
10	Earnings/Common Equity Growth Rate Change	II	12.30	3.52	7.44	9.68	4.80	7.44	3.52	11.86
11	Payout Ratio Growth Rate Change	II	-1.37	-3.98	-4.67	-4.02	-1.96	-6.42	-1.22	-5.55
12	Total Equity Growth Rate Change	II	2.01	-5.71	-5.30	-1.11	5.38	-5.38	-4.00	-1.61
13	Earnings/Total Capital Growth Rate Change	II	11.86	4.61	9.12	9.37	5.99	7.62	5.16	11.86
14	Number of Employees Growth Rate Change	II	2.96	-2.21	-1.70	-.89	-2.63	-3.68	-2.17	2.96
15	Adjusted Stock Price Growth Rate Change	II	-1.68	-3.53	3.94	-1.68	-1.04	-1.04	-6.83	.30
16	Total Debt/Equity Growth Rate Change	II	-.18	-1.25	4.99	-1.25	1.61	1.61	-7.47	.93
17	Earnings/Employee Growth Rate Change	II	15.78	-1.56	7.58	5.28	6.35	7.58	4.69	15.43
18	Adjusted Average Price/Earnings Ratio Change	III	-.06	1.43	.22	-.06	.77	.89	.57	-.11
19	Total Debt/Equity Ratio Change	III	-.06	-.06	-.01	-.05	-.04	-.01	-.05	-.01
20	Payout Ratio Change	III	-.04	.05	.07	-.02	-.08	.05	.05	-.04
21	Price/Equity Ratio Change	III	.86	.60	.17	.52	.39	.38	.60	.39
22	Total Equity Change	III	30.85	31.29	26.19	31.29	23.99	23.99	24.30	32.06
23	Earnings/Total Assets Ratio Change	III	-.01	-.03	-.02	-.02	-.02	-.02	-.02	-.01

TABLE 5-1. (Continued)

Variable Number	Depth of Search		Recognition of Synergy		Attainment of Synergy		Number of Alternatives Evaluated		Depth of Evaluation		Degree of Integration		
	Extensive Search	Limited Search	Recognition Synergy	Not Recog. Synergy	Synergy Attained	Synergy Not Attained	Large Number of Alternatives	Small Number of Alternatives	Thorough Evaluation	Cursory Evaluation	Autonomous	Partial	Complete
1	1.75	-2.38	-1.59	1.10	1.75	-4.52	3.02	4.47	1.75	-2.38	1.36	2.16	-2.38
2	14.08	1.10	7.44	16.52	7.44	8.73	2.28	17.55	8.73	4.39	8.73	4.39	7.44
3	13.71	.67	6.12	16.79	6.12	1.07	1.54	21.23	8.91	2.22	8.88	4.20	5.81
4	-1.01	-1.55	-1.11	-2.08	-.93	-5.88	-2.08	.44	-.09	-1.55	.07	-4.24	-2.31
5	13.58	4.54	5.70	17.66	5.70	9.62	5.04	14.41	9.25	5.42	6.22	6.22	6.22
6	1.73	-2.25	-.01	-8.07	.56	-2.43	-3.63	2.76	1.70	-2.25	1.48	1.73	2.25
7	14.26	1.30	7.29	11.65	8.07	6.62	3.58	20.89	9.52	3.97	9.52	-.01	7.46
8	13.18	.11	7.59	11.39	9.33	6.26	3.70	19.92	11.39	6.26	9.89	-.01	7.72
9	-1.72	-1.90	-1.72	-2.73	-1.72	-6.69	-2.38	.07	-.03	-2.38	-.07	-5.56	-1.72
10	11.86	4.86	5.07	12.00	5.59	7.44	4.86	13.66	9.95	4.86	7.44	5.72	5.07
11	-5.55	-1.37	-2.99	-2.49	-3.35	-2.99	-3.78	-3.35	-4.02	-1.96	-4.02	2.95	-3.89
12	-2.30	-3.64	-1.61	-7.15	-1.11	-2.74	-5.58	1.25	-2.14	-2.74	-2.14	-2.30	-2.74
13	10.07	5.95	5.99	13.17	7.62	8.01	5.16	15.03	9.52	5.99	9.52	3.46	8.88
14	-.89	-2.19	-.89	-3.68	-.72	-1.49	-1.49	.19	2.08	-1.70	.19	2.96	-2.17
15	-.37	-1.68	-2.00	-.37	5.18	-7.24	-2.11	3.94	-1.68	-.37	2.18	-2.00	-2.11
16	-.18	.18	4.04	3.99	-.84	-6.58	-.18	.93	-.18	.70	.70	1.61	5.01
17	14.01	5.01	5.01	8.41	5.01	8.41	4.69	15.78	14.01	6.35	8.59	-2.74	8.59
18	-.11	.93	.28	1.83	.57	.08	.89	-.46	-.06	.77	.57	.89	-.11
19	.02	-.06	-.05	-.04	-.02	-.08	-.06	.02	-.05	-.02	-.01	-.07	-.04
20	-.04	.05	.04	.06	.02	.06	.05	-.06	.00	.06	.04	.02	.05
21	.19	.57	.60	.20	.68	.51	.52	.25	.57	.39	.39	.57	.52
22	26.46	29.55	32.06	16.22	41.17	36.35	23.99	32.06	31.29	26.19	26.46	35.48	20.52
23	-.02	-.02	-.01	-.05	.01	-.03	-.03	.00	-.02	-.02	-.02	-.03	-.02

TABLE 5-1. (Continued)

Variable Number	Objectives Achieved			Changes in Acquisition Program			Existence Type I Plan		Existence Type II Plan		Type of Diversification			
	All	Most	Few	None	Some	Great	Yes	No	Yes	No	Horizontal	Vertical	Concentric	Conglomerate
1	4.03	-.85	-7.39	2.16	-.85	-3.03	2.16	4.52	1.75	-2.86	1.77	.55	-1.59	-3.03
2	9.00	8.73	-14.01	12.71	7.50	4.39	13.55	.50	8.73	1.10	9.41	3.86	7.98	1.10
3	8.88	8.88	-9.93	16.74	4.64	1.54	13.71	-.73	8.91	.67	8.88	4.20	6.84	.67
4	1.55	-1.55	-5.14	-1.55	-.14	-.43	-.43	-1.55	-1.55	-.14	.07	.44	-2.31	-2.08
5	5.42	8.81	-1.83	11.60	8.94	3.12	13.58	3.09	8.94	5.04	9.69	5.42	6.22	8.09
6	2.16	1.41	-8.69	2.64	.56	-6.08	1.70	6.08	1.70	-3.74	1.48	4.90	-2.42	-8.69
7	11.57	6.62	3.46	10.19	7.46	-.01	11.91	3.46	8.09	1.30	8.07	7.29	8.09	11.65
8	9.89	6.26	3.70	11.87	7.59	-2.78	11.87	3.17	9.89	6.26	8.07	7.59	9.33	11.39
9	3.33	-1.87	-9.97	-2.38	-1.72	-1.68	-1.29	-1.90	-1.87	-1.68	-1.68	-.03	-1.90	-2.73
10	5.59	5.72	2.31	12.00	5.72	3.34	11.38	1.80	9.68	4.86	5.72	4.86	5.59	12.00
11	9.01	-5.13	-2.99	-5.55	-1.37	2.95	-3.98	-2.99	-4.02	-1.04	-3.35	12.50	-1.37	-12.94
12	1.77	-4.00	-7.59	-3.86	-2.30	-3.64	-1.61	-3.64	-1.61	-3.64	-2.61	4.30	-.86	-7.15
13	8.88	9.28	-1.18	10.91	5.95	1.72	9.52	5.99	9.39	5.99	8.88	3.46	8.01	13.17
14	1.46	-1.49	-3.03	.19	-1.67	-1.49	.19	-2.63	-.99	-2.21	.19	4.10	-1.49	-5.23
15	21.36	-4.54	-17.37	5.18	-.36	-8.51	-.36	-2.00	-2.11	-.37	5.18	21.36	-4.11	-.37
16	-4.04	.70	-.18	.78	-4.04	1.61	.18	-1.25	-5.01	2.45	2.48	-.84	-7.05	3.99
17	11.05	5.28	-9.03	5.28	8.41	4.69	9.24	1.69	5.01	7.58	8.59	2.36	5.28	8.41
18	-.32	.57	1.08	.89	1.97	.28	-.11	.89	-.11	.89	.28	.89	-.06	1.83
19	-.02	-.07	-.09	.02	-.04	-.06	-.06	-.04	-.06	-.04	.00	.05	.08	.01
20	-.04	.05	.08	.00	.05	.04	-.04	.07	-.03	.08	.04	.05	-.03	.06
21	.39	.52	.31	.52	.52	.39	.31	.52	.52	.39	.52	1.47	.86	.20
22	16.39	35.48	31.29	32.06	36.35	26.19	26.46	29.55	30.85	26.19	26.19	90.44	35.44	15.95
23	.00	-.02	-.03	-.02	-.01	-.02	-.02	-.02	-.02	-.02	-.03	.00	-.01	-.03

93

TABLE 5-1. (Continued)

Variable Number	Type of Synergy			Type of Problems Encountered				Price Determination			Formal Acquisition Budget	
	Market	Technology	Other	Integration	Synergy	Personnel	Market	Outside Appraisal	Market Value	E (Future Profit)	Yes	No
1	-2.14	-4.26	1.36	-4.52	10.12	-4.52	-5.66	-4.52	-3.02	-1.59	-3.03	-2.14
2	7.50	7.40	7.98	9.41	14.08	1.10	3.86	7.98	7.98	7.50	7.40	7.98
3	6.12	4.64	6.84	9.09	13.71	2.22	4.20	6.84	6.81	6.81	4.64	6.84
4	-1.11	-2.31	.44	-5.14	-12.03	-2.10	-5.05	-2.09	-1.11	-1.01	-2.10	-1.15
5	8.81	5.42	6.22	9.69	11.60	8.81	5.04	9.25	3.12	9.25	5.70	8.09
6	-1.41	-2.43	-.01	-5.63	-11.06	-8.16	-8.07	-8.16	-3.63	-.06	-2.43	-1.41
7	7.29	7.29	9.25	7.29	14.26	-1.58	7.29	7.29	3.97	7.29	7.46	7.29
8	7.59	6.26	9.33	7.59	13.48	-2.47	7.59	7.59	9.33	7.59	4.65	7.72
9	-1.72	-1.90	1.35	-5.56	-14.03	-2.73	-5.56	-2.73	-1.87	-1.40	-2.45	-1.87
10	5.72	5.07	6.48	10.47	11.38	7.88	7.44	7.88	5.59	6.48	5.72	6.48
11	-4.67	-2.99	-5.13	-8.42	-15.13	-8.00	-2.99	3.33	-4.02	-3.35	-3.98	-3.35
12	-2.61	-.89	-.89	-2.74	-10.00	-5.38	-4.00	-.63	-3.64	-2.30	-1.11	-3.64
13	5.99	5.95	9.12	5.99	8.01	7.43	8.01	7.42	9.39	5.99	8.01	7.62
14	-.21	-1.67	-.89	-2.21	-9.32	-1.49	-1.49	-5.96	-2.19	-1.49	-2.19	-.89
15	-1.04	-3.53	-4.11	-3.53	-24.70	-5.83	-13.07	-4.11	2.18	-1.04	-4.11	2.18
16	.18	-7.05	-6.42	-.18	-24.42	1.61	-6.58	-.18	-1.25	-.18	-9.35	.18
17	7.58	8.59	8.79	5.28	15.43	2.36	7.58	6.35	5.01	8.41	5.01	6.35
18	.08	-.06	.28	-1.25	-.75	1.43	.93	-.02	1.42	.22	-1.12	.77
19	-.02	-.09	-.02	-.09	-.01	-.04	-.09	-.02	-.04	-.05	-.08	-.02
20	.05	.05	-.03	.06	.06	.09	.04	.00	.04	.04	.02	.04
21	.57	1.01	.60	.39	.39	.52	.60	.39	1.04	.38	1.38	.38
22	26.19	49.54	35.48	29.55	26.46	31.77	31.29	37.32	37.32	26.46	40.39	21.63
23	-.02	-.01	-.01	-.02	-.01	-.02	-.02	-.00	-.01	-.02	-.01	-.03

TABLE 5-1. (Continued)

Variable Number	Actual vs. Sales			Forecast Profit			Performance Profit Margin		
	Less Than	Equal To	Greater Than	Less Than	Equal To	Greater Than	Less Than	Equal To	Greater Than
1	-6.94	.55	1.31	-4.52	1.75	1.33	-4.26	-2.14	1.33
2	.31	12.71	9.00	1.10	7.50	11.76	3.86	7.44	12.32
3	.67	16.74	9.09	.67	8.91	11.71	4.20	8.88	13.71
4	-5.14	-1.11	.44	-5.14	-1.11	1.55	-4.24	-2.44	2.62
5	1.64	21.01	9.69	3.09	6.22	12.04	5.04	6.22	13.52
6	-8.16	.54	1.70	-3.74	1.73	1.70	-2.43	-.06	1.70
7	1.30	9.52	11.57	.10	9.52	11.91	3.46	9.52	14.26
8	3.70	11.87	9.89	.11	11.87	11.86	4.65	9.34	13.42
9	-2.53	-1.87	-.71	-7.34	-1.87	2.73	-6.53	-1.87	2.73
10	4.80	8.42	7.88	4.80	8.42	11.37	5.59	6.48	11.86
11	-2.99	-5.55	-3.98	-1.96	-3.98	-3.35	-3.35	-6.42	1.37
12	-1.13	-.63	-1.11	-5.71	-.89	-.10	-2.74	-.89	-1.61
13	3.46	9.52	8.88	5.95	9.52	9.28	5.16	9.52	9.39
14	-3.03	2.08	-.89	-3.56	5.68	-.89	-2.63	-.99	-1.49
15	-3.53	-2.11	5.18	-4.11	-.36	19.84	-4.54	-.36	19.84
16	-1.25	.18	.93	-2.85	1.19	-.84	-1.25	-.84	.93
17	-1.56	4.69	14.01	1.48	4.69	15.29	-1.56	8.79	15.43
18	1.42	-.75	.72	1.08	-.75	.72	.93	.57	-.02
19	-.09	-.05	.00	-.09	-.02	.02	-.07	-.04	.03
20	.09	-.05	.02	.05	.00	.02	.04	.04	-.06
21	1.01	.31	.52	.68	1.19	.29	.57	1.04	.19
22	31.77	20.52	26.43	31.27	95.84	26.19	31.29	53.91	2.51
23	-.03	-.06	-.01	-.03	.00	-.01	-.03	-.02	-.02

I. Degree of Obtainment of Objectives

During the course of this study, a question was raised whether executives' perceptions of their achievement were a good indicator of the actual financial performance of the firm. A comparison of questionnaire responses with the actual post-acquisition performance of the firm yields a measure of the accuracy of the executives' perceptions. We found that the executives' indication of achievement is a very reliable measure of the firm's actual performance. For example, in those firms whose executives indicated that all or most of the firm's objectives had been achieved, the median change in earnings/share growth rate was plus 9.89 and 6.26 percentage points respectively, while it was only 3.70 percentage points for those firms having indicated that few objectives had been obtained. Without specifically citing the data, the case was the same for most performance measures which can be considered as proper objectives for the firm with the notable exception of the price/earnings ratios.

The paradoxical behavior of price/earnings (the higher the degree of attainment of objectives, the lower the price/earnings ratio) suggests that the ratio is not an important objective for most managers. Since greater positive change in earnings growth is accompanied by post-acquisition price/earnings ratios, it would appear that earnings growth was the dominant objective.

On the other hand, there is a very strong correlation of stock price to the number of objectives achieved. Those firms acknowledging total success had a median change of +21.36 percentage points in stock price growth; those succeeding in most of their objectives, a median change of -4.54; and those not succeeding, a negative change of -17.37 percentage points. This suggests that stock price rather than price/earnings was the executives' yardstick for judging success.

II. Planning

The presence of all four planning variables was highly correlated with performance, specifically sales, earnings, earnings/common equity, earnings/total capital, and debt/equity ratio. They were most highly correlated with earnings on common equity and earnings on total assets. The debt/equity ratio decreased as the degree of planning increased. This is a very strong indication that planning pays off in terms of superior results. Further proof of this appears later in this chapter.

Very interestingly, payout was an inverse function of planning; the more planning activity, the lower the post-acquisition payout.

III. Search

As we might expect, from the relationship of search to planning, the depth and direction of search was also intimately associated with increased performance. A few typical results are shown below in Table 5-2.

Table 5-1 illustrates very vividly the impact of directed, extensive search on profits and efficiency and to a lesser extent on stock price growth. Debt-equity change is inversely related to search. Dividend payout percentage, although not listed above, is negatively related to search.

TABLE 5-2

THE RELATIONSHIP OF SEARCH ACTIVITIES AND PERFORMANCE

| | CHANGE IN VARIABLE | | | | |
| | Type of Search | | | Depth of Search | |
Performance Variable	Passive	Broad-cast	Directed	Exten-sive	Limited
Sales Growth Rate II	-3.74	-3.63	2.69	1.75	-7.25
Earnings/Share Rate II	3.17	3.70	15.06	13.48	.11
Earnings/Total Capital Rate II	7.62	5.16	11.86	10.07	5.95
Stock Price Growth Rate II	-1.04	-5.83	0.30	-.37	-1.68
Total Debt/Equity Ratio III	-.01	-.05	-.01	.02	-.06

IV. Evaluation of Alternatives

A very interesting result is that firms evaluating only a *small* number of potential acquisitions performed very much better than those looking at a multitude of alternatives.

When combined with the depth of evaluation, a small number of alternatives which were thoroughly evaluated seemed to be the recipe for success. *In fact, of all twenty-one questionnaire variables tested, these two characteristics gave the most consistently strong relationship to success.*

Thus, there would appear to be strong normative implications for placing emphasis on carefully selecting and thoroughly evaluating a small subset of all the alternatives brought to the firm's attention.

V. Integration

For the great majority of statistical tests run, integration was found to have little influence on growth or performance. The strongest statement concerning integration that the results will allow us to make is that partial integration tends to produce the poorest performance. Apparently, the firm should try for complete integration of its acquisitions, or it should let them remain autonomous. Although the sales growth rate change for all three degrees of integration was approximately equal, earnings and earnings per share mildly favored either autonomy or complete integration. But even this conclusion is only weakly suggested by the statistics. This result is not surprising in view of the short post-acquisition period over which we measured our results.

VI. Synergy

Previously, we noted the lack of correspondence between prior recognition and the eventual attainment of synergy. Testing synergy questions against performance again brought this out. In fact, a weak case may be made for the relative superiority in performance of those firms which did not consciously recognize the potential synergistic effects beforehand, particularly insofar as the efficiency variables, earnings/total capital and earnings/common equity are concerned.

The attainment of synergy had little relationship to most measures of performance, with two exceptions. The change in the growth rate of the total stock of assets for firms attaining synergy was only -.43 percentage points, as compared to a -5.88 percentage points for those firms attaining no synergistic effects. Second, there was a very marked difference in the adjusted stock price growth rate changes between the two groups. Synergistic firms had a positive 5.18 change, while firms without the synergistic benefits had a -7.24 percentage point change. Since earnings-per-share performance was neutral, insofar as synergy was concerned, this implies that the market attached a higher post-acquisition price/earnings multiple to firms reaping synergistic benefits. Indeed, on an adjusted basis, these firms averaged slightly better than a half-point increase in their price/earnings ratio, while those firms not attaining synergy had essentially no change in their price/earnings multiple.

VII. Change in Acquisition Program

One of the questions included in the questionnaire was whether the firm had altered its acquisition program based on its previous experience. By comparing the responses to this question with the responses to the number of objectives achieved and the actual post-acquisition performance, we obtained an indication of the motivations for a change in the acquisition program. Firms which exhibited unsatisfactory performance, particularly in sales, earnings, and stock price growth, were generally quick to alter their approach to acquisitions. An interesting corollary to the question of change would be to find whether these firms moved toward systematic acquisition planning. Unfortunately, our questionnaire was not constructed so as to yield this information. Nonetheless, it is noteworthy that firms actually recognized their inadequacies in the acquisition programs and took steps to improve them.

SECTION 2: DOES PLANNING PAY?

A question of great interest to us is whether systematic planning "paid off" in terms of superior financial performance. To answer this, we compared the change in performance of the 22 "planners," which exhibited at least 6 of the 8 strong planning, search, and evaluation characteristics, against the rest of the questionnarie sample. The results were impressive. Tables 5-3 and 5-4 and Figures 5-1 through 5-6 summarize our findings.

Table 5-3 gives the value of the test statistic for each comparison and the median change in the performance variable for both groups of firms. It shows that, on virtually every measure of performance, the planners turned in much better performance, as measured by the respective medians of the samples.

A comparison of means and the associated standard deviations is given in Table 5-4. *Note that in each case (with the notable exception of price/earnings ratio) the change in performance for the "planners" is larger than that for the rest of the sample, and additionally, that its variance of change is, in all but one case, less than that for the "planners."* Thus, not only did the firms with formal planning systems perform better, but there was less variation in their results. *The systematic planning, search, and evaluation approach not only produced better results on the average, but also produced more predictable results.* This should be welcomed information to all firms that are looking toward acquisitions as a means of growth but desire a minimal degree of risk.

Let us examine earnings per share, stock price, and the capital efficiency ratios shown in Table 5-4.

Earnings per Share Growth. By either method of measuring growth, Class I or Class II, planners outperform the others, for the increase from pre- to post-acquisition in the earnings-per-share growth rate was 14.01 percentage points for the planners, with a standard deviation of 30.28, while that of the rest of the sample was only 1.79 percentage points with a

TABLE 5-3

ANALYSIS OF COMPARATIVE PERFORMANCE OF FIRMS
DISPLAYING CONSISTENT ACQUISITION APPROACH
VS. REMAINDER OF QUESTIONNAIRE FIRMS

Performance Variable	Value of Test Statistic	Median Group I	Median Group II
Sales Growth I	2.50 *	2.25	-2.06
Earnings Growth I	3.25 *	14.08	2.26
Earnings/Share Growth I	3.32 *	13.71	2:22
Total Assets Growth I	-.39	.19	1.34
Earnings/Common Equity Growth I	2.47 *	14.00	3.98
Sales Growth II	2.82 *	2.64	-6.08
Earnings Growth II	3.00 *	17.51	.05
Earnings/Share Growth II	3.35 *	16.70	-1.24
Total Assets Growth II	.43	-1.00	-2.55
Earnings/Common Equity Growth II	3.11 *	12.08	3.43
Payout Ratio Growth II	-.06	-5.21	-3.14
Total Equity Growth II	1.96 *	-.86	-5.40
Earnings/Total Capital Growth II	2.88 *	10.97	4.47
Stock Price Growth (Adjusted)	1.82 *	-.03	-7.33
Debt/Equity Growth II	-.23	-2.11	-.33
Price/Earnings Ratio III	-2.19 *	-.28	.98
Debt/Equity Ratio III	1.36	.00	-.06
Payout Ratio III	-2.30 *	-.04	.06
Price/Equity Ratio III	-.59	.18	.52
Total Equity III	-.73	23.49	31.52
Earnings/Total Equity III	1.61	-.01	-.03

Number in sample of firms with consistent behavior = 22
Number of remaining firms   = 40
*Indicates Significance at the .05 level (95% confidence level)

standard deviation of 68.06, a result which could occur randomly less than
five times in a thousand.

Stock-Price Growth. The adjusted stock-price growth rate for the ideal
firms was increased by 7.77 percentage points, while that of the firms with
random behavior decreased by 10.42 percentage points. Again, the standard
deviation calculations reflect the greater predictability of the results for the
sample of planners.

Efficiency Variables. Although not so pronounced as the earnings/share
results, the relative increments in growth rates of earnings/common equity

TABLE 5-4

COMPARISON OF MEANS AND STANDARD DEVIATIONS
OF PERFORMANCE MEASURES FOR "IDEAL" FIRMS
AND THOSE WITH RANDOM BEHAVIOR

Performance Variable	MEANS		STANDARD DEVIATIONS	
	Ideal Firms	Others	Ideal Firms	Others
Sales Growth Rate Change I	2.75	-.63	12.62	9.25
Earnings Growth Rate Change I	13.14	10.86	31.62	45.13
Earnings/Share Growth Rate Change I	12.83	9.98	32.44	44.01
Total Assets Growth Rate Change I	-.64	.57	6.42	8.54
Earnings/Common Equity Growth Rate Change I	11.39	10.52	28.63	40.21
Sales Growth Rate Change II	-.82	-11.18	17.91	24.60
Earnings Growth Rate Change II	13.61	2.03	32.33	72.10
Earnings/Share Growth Rate Change II	14.01	1.79	30.28	68.06
Total Assets Growth Rate Change II	-5.16	-8.93	13.05	25.68
Earnings/Common Equity Growth Rate Change II	12.28	8.45	21.68	54.63
Payout Ratio Growth Rate Change II	3.34	-3.80	14.96	27.77
Total Equity Growth Rate Change II	-1.22	-7.61	7.86	15.33
Earnings/Total Capital Growth Rate Change II	12.80	7.15	24.47	50.91
Adjusted Stock Price Growth Rate Change II	7.77	-10.42	32.53	45.21
Debt/Equity Growth Rate Change II	-6.00	-1.85	16.79	18.86
Price/Earnings Ratio Change III	-.16	2.07	2.29	5.54
Debt/Equity Ratio Change III	.00	-.10	.17	.27
Payout Ratio Change III	-.02	.15	.14	.60
Price/Equity Ratio Change III	.70	.80	.91	.94
Total Equity Change III	58.91	67.77	95.65	127.34
Earnings/Total Equity Ratio Change III	-.02	-.03	.04	.04

and earnings/total capital, when measured by Class II yardsticks, between the planners and the rest of the sample was approximately 50%, with the standard deviation for the planners being less than half that for the rest of the sample.

As noted before, the effect of acquisitions has been earnings/total capital; however, this tendency is slightly less (or the reduction on average is less) for the consistent planners.

Price/Earnings. The lone inconsistency in our results is the relative behavior of the price/earnings ratios of the two samples. Here we note that the nonplanning acquirers experienced a mean increase of more than two percentage points, while the planners had an actual small decrease of .16 percentage points. The adverse nature of the price/earnings ratios is consistent, however, with the over all behavior of this variable discussed in Chapter 3. It suggests that, while planning pays off in economic results, it is still either not visible enough or not considered important enough by the investing public.

Interestingly, the investment community was consistent in this view, since the standard deviation for the planners was smaller than for nonplanners.

Graphic Displays. Since mean and variance analysis is only a partial comparison of two distributions, we have plotted complete distributions for sales, earnings, and earnings/share, stock price, price/earnings, and earnings/total capital on Figures 5-1 through 5-6. From these graphs, it is easy to see the very clear dominance of results obtained by planners over nonplanners—except, again, for price/earnings leaving little doubt as to the benefit of systematic planning to acquisition practice.

Summary.

Two of the authors of this study are active practitioners and consultants on formal corporate planning. It is, therefore, with great interest, but also with special care that we sought a relation between use of organized planning and success of acquisition activity.

In this chapter we presented three different tests: (1) correlation between individual planning attributes and the degree of improvement in performance of acquiring firms; (2) statistical comparison of means and variances of performance improvements of "ideal" planners with nonplanners or partial planners; and (3) graphical plots of the distribution of improvements in performance for the three groups. All three tests point to a strong conclusion that the planners performed better on the average and with a smaller spread around the average than did the nonplanners on all important performance variables except one. Ironically, that one was the price/earnings ratio—a measure of the recognition given to the firm by the investment community.

To the best of our knowledge, as this is written, this is the first quantitative and statistically significant test to show that formal planning does pay.

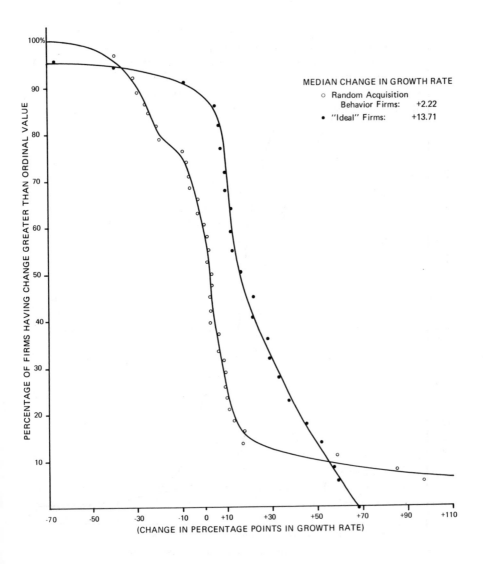

Fig. 5-1.
Comparative Distribution of Change in Growth Rate of
Earnings/Share between "Ideal" Firms and Firms
with Random Acquisition Behavior.

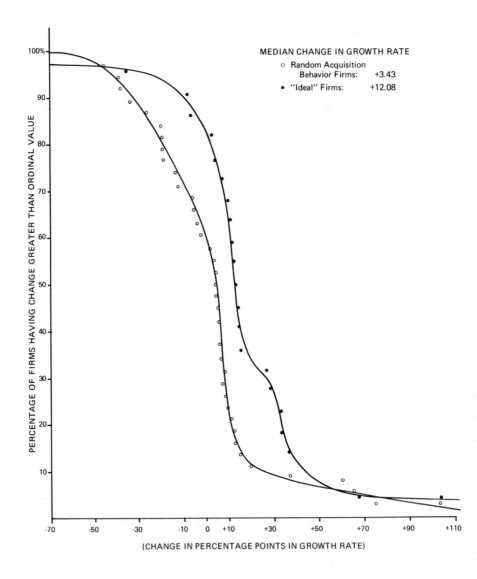

Fig. 5-2.
Comparative Distribution of Change in Growth Rate of
Stock Price between "Ideal" Firms and Firms with
Random Acquisition Behavior.

104

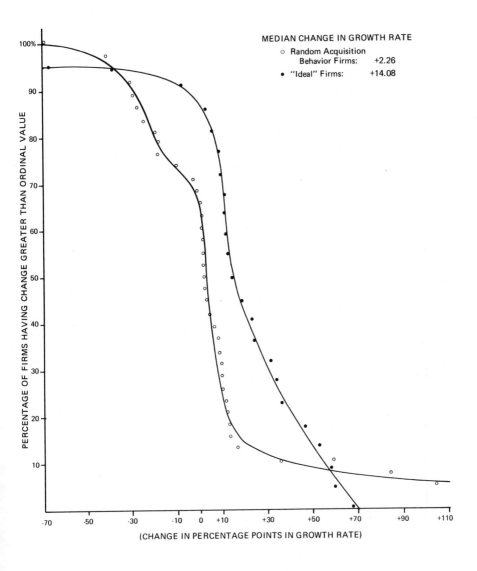

Fig. 5-3.
Comparative Distribution of Change in Growth Rate of
Earnings between "Ideal" Firms and Firms with
Random Acquisition Behavior.

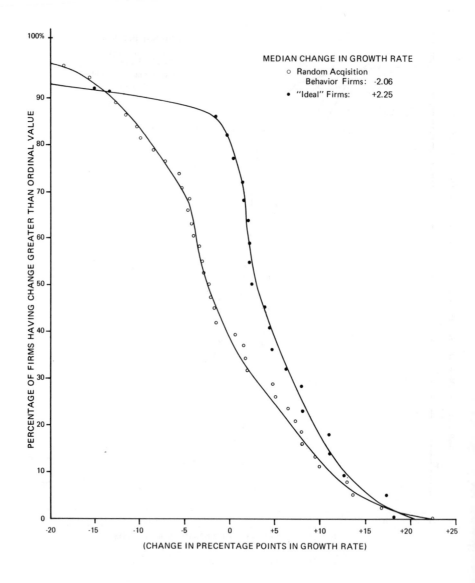

Fig. 5-4.
Comparative Distribution of Change in Growth Rate of
Sales between "Ideal" Firms and Firms with
Random Acquisition Behavior.

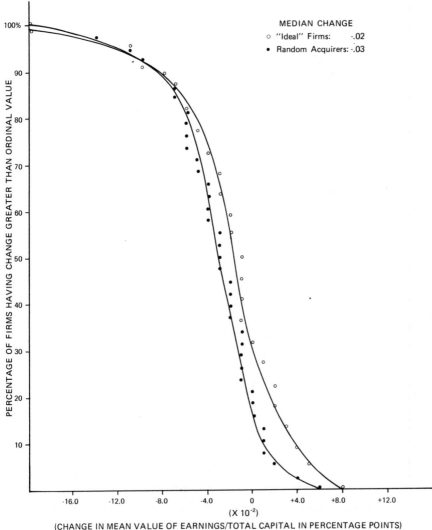

Fig. 5-5.
Comparative Distribution of Change in Mean Value of
Earnings/Total Capital between "Ideal" Firms and
Firms with Random Behavior.

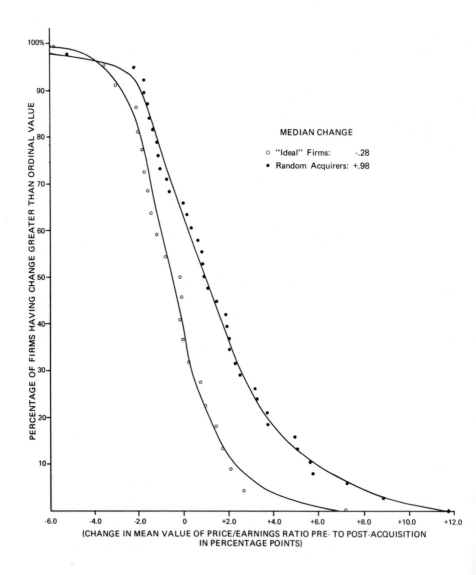

Fig. 5-6.
Comparative Distribution of Change in Mean Level of
P/E Ratio between "Ideal" Firms and Firms with
Random Acquisition Behavior.

Appendix A
QUESTIONNAIRE DESIGN

The questionnaire was sent in two very similar forms—one for firms whose program included only one acquisition and another for those with multiple-acquisition programs. Because of the high degree of similarity, only the multiple-acquisition version is included in this appendix.

The numbers in the response blanks indicate the number of respondents who checked that response. If a similar question existed on the single-acquisition version, its number of responses is coded with (s) for single-acquisition respondents and (m) for multiple-acquisition respondents.

Carnegie-Mellon University Schenley Park
Pittsburgh, Pennsylvania 15213
[412] 621-2600

Questionnaire Cover Letter

Dear

We are conducting a study sponsored by the McKinsey Foundation for Management
Research. The purpose of the study is to examine strategic planning and decision-making
in business firms. The study is an attempt to learn from the extensive experience of
industrial leaders about the successful patterns of business behavior and the associated
role of strategic planning.

To do the study, we need your assistance in having the enclosed questionnaire completed.
Your response will be treated as highly confidential, and the report which results from
this study will not associate any of the findings with the responding firms. Copies of
the report will be sent to all respondents.

We have attempted to minimize the effort which is required to provide the needed data
by presenting the questionnaire in the form of a checklist. The questionnaire
consists of two parts: Part I will best be completed by someone who was directly involved in the concerned acquisition activity. This part will require only a few minutes
to answer. The questions on Part II require some historical data and will best
be completed by a staff analyst.

We would very much appreciate your co-operation. If possible, would you please
return each part in its enclosed envelope within two weeks.

Sincerely yours,

H. Igor Ansoff
Professor of Industrial Administration

Multiple-Acquisition Program Questionnaire

ACQUISITION QUESTIONNAIRE

PART 1

Firm Code _____

Your firm has had a period of acquisition activity which is of particular interest to our study. This period started with the acquisition of_____ in 19___ and ended with the acquisition of_____ in 19___.Would you please answer the following questions with regard to that period. Any other comments or clarifications you might wish to make about your merger program would also be appreciated.

1. At the start of the period, did your firm have a formal statement of objectives (for example, a target growth rate of sales)?

   Yes _*12 (S)*_ _*27 (M)*_   No _*26 (S)*_ _*28 (M)*_

   If yes, skip to number 4.

2. Was a formal statement of objectives for the firm adopted during the period?

   Yes _*5*_   No _*26*_

   If no, skip to number 7.

3. At what point in the period were the objectives established?

   Early _*3*_   Midway _*2*_   Late _*1*_

4. Did this statement include an explicit growth objective?

   Yes _*9 (S)*_ _*20 (M)*_   No _*4 (S)*_ _*11 (M)*_

   If no, skip to number 7.

5. Was there a management decision which specified a preferred method for securing the major portion of this growth objective (for example, acquisition, licensing, or internal development of new products)?

   Yes _*9 (S)*_ _*16 (M)*_   No _*2 (S)*_ _*7 (M)*_

   If no, skip to number 7.

6. What was the planned method for attaining the desired growth?
    (If more than one, please indicate the order of importance).

    A. Expansion of current markets with existing products _____25_____

    B. Finding new markets for existing products   _____10_____

    C. Developing new products the better to satisfy demand
       of existing markets   _____25_____

    D. Developing new products for new markets   _____20_____

    E. Other (Please specify.) _____   _____4_____

7. With regard to the concerned acquisition period, where, if ever,
    were specific plans and criteria established for acquiring or
    merging?

    A. Before the period   _____17_____

    B. Early in the period   _____12_____

    C. Midway in the period   _____2_____

    D. Late in the period   _____0_____

    E. After the period   _____12_____

    F. None yet established   _____7_____

8. Which of the following, if any, were reasons for the concerned
    acquisitions? (Please indicate the order of importance.)

                                                             55 (S)*
    A. To complete product lines   104 (M)

                                                             22 (S)
    B. To meet demands of diversified customers   23 (M)

                                                             15 (S)
    C. To acquire goodwill, prestige, or brand names   15 (M)

                                                             17 (S)
    D. To increase control of sales outlets   22 (M)

                                                              8 (S)
    E. To reduce dependence on one or few customers   26 (M)

                                                             20 (S)
    F. To reduce dependence on suppliers   18 (M)

    G. To offset unsatisfactory sales growth   25 (S)
          in present markets   45 (M)

    H. To offset unsatisfactory profit margins   13 (S)
          in present markets   13 (M)

I. To increase market share

45 (S)
57 (M)

J. To offset technological obsolescence of facilities

0 (S)
0 (M)

K. To obtain patents, licenses, or technological
   knowledge

23 (S)
30 (M)

L. To utilize waste or by-products

0 (S)
1 (M)

M. To capitalize on existing distinctive technological
   expertise

22 (S)
42 (M)

N. To capitalize on distinctive managerial talents

7 (S)
23 (M)

O. To fully utilize existing production capacity

22 (S)
21 (M)

P. To fully utilize existing marketing capabilities,
   contacts, or channels

28 (S)
45 (M)

Q. To attain a minimum size needed for efficient
   research and development

5 (S)
2 (M)

R. To attain a minimum size needed for effective
   advertising methods

0 (S)
3 (M)

S. To attain a minimum size needed for listing on
   a stock exchange

0 (S)
1 (M)

T. Other (Please specify.) _____

32 (S)
53 (M)

*Five-point scale

9. Of the firms acquired during the concerned period, what proportion fall into each of the following categories with regard to the party who initiated contact between the firms?

Acquirer *20 (S)* *3865/45 (M)*   Acquiree *9 (S)* *1110/17 (M)*   Other *7 (S)* *225/4 (M)*

10. At any time during the concerned period, was there intensive search for acquisition or merger possibilities?

Yes *17 (S)* *22 (M)*   No *21 (S)* *31 (M)*

If no, skip to number 16.

11. Was this search activity a continual process throughout the period?

    Yes ____22____   No ___5___

12. Who was in charge of the search?

    A. Chairman of the Board   *2 (S)*
                                                               4 (M)

    B. President   *10 (S)*
                                                               8 (M)

    C. Executive or Administrative Vice-President   *1 (S)*
                                                               7 (M)

    D. Other Vice-President   *6 (S)*
                                                               10 (M)

    E. Special Staff Director   *2 (S)*
                                                               5 (M)

    F. Other (Please specify.) _____   *2 (M)*

13. What method of search was used to locate acquisition possibilities?

    A. Use of outside agencies and brokers   *5 (S) **
                                                               30 (M)

    B. Broadcasting of your acquisition interest to   *7 (S)*
       pertinent parties   *20 (M)*

    C. Analysis by a special staff to uncover desirable   *3 (S)*
       candidates   *38 (M)*

    D. Wait for other interested parties to come to you   *3 (S)*
                                                               12 (M)

    E. Contact through business associates   *7 (S)*
                                                               34 (M)

    F. Other (Please specify.) _____   *2 (S)*
                                                               4 (M)

    *Three point scale

14. About how many acquisition possibilities were uncovered by the search, i.e., passed a preliminary screening process?

    292/13 = 22.4 (S)
    1559/23 = 67.8 (M)

15. During the period, what was the approximate average number of people whose primary responsibility was the finding and evaluating of acquisition possibilities?

    Full-time _*36/16 = 2.25*_ Part-time ___*74/19 = 3.9*___

16. When seeking acquisition possibilities, did you look for a "common thread" or "synergy," i.e., a close relation between the firms?

Yes _20 (S)_ / _44 (M)_   No _12 (S)_ / _8 (M)_

If no, skip to number 19.

17. What was the most common nature of the above close relation? (Please indicate order if more than one.)

A. Common sales administration, warehousing, or distribution channels — _13 (S) *_ / _48 (M)_

B. Common types of facilities or personnel skills — _10 (S)_ / _25 (M)_

C. Common raw materials or products — _14 (S)_ / _36 (M)_

D. Common technology or R & D — _4 (S)_ / _53 (M)_

E. Common types of needed cometencies of top-level management — _10 (S)_ / _30 (M)_

F. Other (Please specify.) _____ — _2 (S)_ / _17 (M)_

18. For the firms acquired during the concerned period, how have the post-acquisition benefits which were derived from this close relation compared to your expectations? (Please indicate the approximate proportion of firms in each category.)

Higher _8 (S)_ / _1238/17 (M)_   Same _8 (S)_ / _1715/22 (M)_   Lower _8 (S)_ / _1646/23 (M)_

19. Which of the following changes, if any, have occurred in the acquisition search-and-evaluation activity since the concerned acquisition period?

A. A change in objectives — _14 (S)_ / _26 (M)_

B. A change in organizational responsibility — _17 (S)_ / _24 (M)_

C. A change in staffing of the activity — _19 (S)_ / _28 (M)_

D. A change in the characteristics of desirable acquisition candidates — _14 (S)_ / _23 (M)_

E. Other (Please specify.) _____ — _7 (M)_

20. How consistent was the manner and extent of the organizational integration after the acquisition across all of the acquired firms?

A. Very similar integration processes   _14_

B. Similar in most important aspects   _15_

C. Widely divergent integration processes   _19_

   If C, please skip to number 25.

21. Was a separate executive or group given responsibility for the majority of the post-acquisition integration activities?

                    18 (S)   19 (M)
          Yes   _15 (M)_   No   _20 (M)_

If no, please skip to number 23.

22. What was the position in the organization held by the person or group responsible for the majority of the integration activities?

A. President   _5 (S)_
                                           _6 (M)_

B. Board   _2 (S)_
                                           _2 (M)_

C. Vice-president   _15 (S)_
                                           _12 (M)_

D. Special staff position   _5 (S)_
                                           _2 (M)_

E. Other (Please specify.) _____   _1 (S)_
                                           _0 (M)_

23. For the concerned acquisitions, what responsibility for integration decisions was given to the acquired firm? (Please indicate the approximate proportion of firms in each category.)

A. A portion of the responsibility was about proportional   _13 (S)_
   to the relative sizes of the firms   _12 (M)_

B. Little or no responsibility   _11 (S)_
                                           _14 (M)_

C. About equal responsibility with acquiring firm   _11 (S)_
                                                     _9 (M)_

D. Other (Please specify.) _____   _2 (S)_
                                           _0 (M)_

24. What degree of integration was originally intended for the acquired firm? (Please indicate the proportion of firms in each category.)

A. Completely autonomous operation
$\frac{17\ (S)}{1433/17\ (M)}$

B. Highly integrated functional areas
$\frac{5\ (S)}{725/8\ (M)}$

C. Uniform policies and procedures
$\frac{10\ (S)}{775/11\ (M)}$

D. Integrated in all activities
$\frac{5\ (S)}{617/9\ (M)}$

E. Other (Please specify.) _____
$\frac{1\ (S)}{150/2\ (M)}$

25. To what degree were the major objectives accomplished for the acquisitions of the concerned period? (Please indicate the proportion of firms whose contributions are approximated by each category.)

A. All objectives satisfied
$\frac{11\ (S)}{805/11\ (M)}$

B. Most objectives satisfied
$\frac{16\ (S)}{3623/41\ (M)}$

C. Few objectives satisfied
$\frac{9\ (S)}{567/10\ (M)}$

D. No degree satisfied
$\frac{2\ (S)}{130/2\ (M)}$

26. If major problems occurred which hindered the attainment of the initial objectives of the program, which of the following, if any, were contributing factors?

A. Unanticipated integration problems
$\frac{5\ (S)}{11\ (M)}$

B. Personnel problems
$\frac{15\ (S)}{23\ (M)}$

C. Legal problems
$\frac{1\ (S)}{1\ (M)}$

D. Perceived "common thread" did not materialize
$\frac{3\ (S)}{7\ (M)}$

E. Market potentials did not materialize
$\frac{11\ (S)}{21\ (M)}$

F. Other (Please specify.) _____
$\frac{1\ (S)}{3\ (M)}$

Do we have your permission to acknowledge your co-operation in any reports of this study? (Care will be exercised to assure that there will be no possibility of identifying individual firms with any portion of the results.)

Yes _____   No_____

Would you like a summary report of the findings of the study?

Yes _____   No_____

Would you please give us the name of the person who will fill out the second part of the questionnaire so that we might get in touch with him if any questions arise.

Mr. _____

Thank you for your co-operation.

ACQUISITION QUESTIONNAIRE

PART II

Firm Code _____

Would you please provide the following data with regard to your acquisi-

tion activity between 19___and 19___. The period of interest started with

your acquisition of _____ and

ended with your acquisition of _____ .

1. What was the financial vehicle used for the acquisitions? (Please
    indicate the proportion of firms within each category.)

    A. Entirely cash
    _21 (S)_
    _33 (M)_

    B. Entirely common stock
    _9 (S)_
    _14 (M)_

    C. A mixture of cash and stock
    _3 (S)_
    _16 (M)_

    D. Other (Please explain.) _____
    _2 (S)_
    _4 (M)_

2. For the concerned acquisitions, what were the most important
    considerations in the determination of the price of the acquired
    firm? (Please indicate the proportion of firms within each
    category.)

    A. Use of outside appraisal
    _283/7 = 40.5%_

    B. Market value
    _1690/23 = 73.5%_

    C. Expected future profitability
    _2623/33 = 79.5%_

    D. Value of patents, licenses, etc.
    _103/3 = 34.3%_

    E. Other (Please specify.) _____
    _120/2 = 60%_

3. Does the acquisition activity (search and evaluation of acquisition alternatives) presently have a formal annual budget assigned to it?

	4 (S)		30 (S)
Yes	8 (M)	No	42 (M)

    If yes, what is the approximate amount? _600,000/4_

4. What was the approximate annual budget for the acquisition activity for the years immediately before and after the concerned period?

    Before _$ 425,000/4_   After _$ 575,000/5_

5. For the concerned acquisitions, on the average, how many prospects were subjected to an evaluation which required more than one man-month of effort?

    (M) 380/33 Range: 0 (15 values of zero) to 300
    (S) 42/29 Range: 0 to 15

6. For each of the concerned acquisitions, what was the average number of acquisition prospects for which there were extensive negotiations without acquisition consummation?

    (M) 41/35 Range: 0 (21 values) to 10
    (S) 129/30 Range: 0 to 100

7. What was the average length of time from the first recognition of an acquired firm as a prospect until the closing of the acquisition?

    (M) 27.2 years/45 ≈ 6 months Range: 1 month to 2 years
    (S) 26.4 years/32 ≈ 10.5 months average. Range: 1 month to 5 years

8. What degree of change, if any, is currently being planned for the acquisition activity of your firm?

A. No change	15 (S)
	21 (M)
B. Minor change	5 (S)
	7 (M)
C. Substantial change	14 (S)
	15 (M)

9. What are the organizational statuses of the acquired firms? (Please indicate the proportion of firms within each category.)

A. Partially-owned subsidiary   _333/5 = 66.7%_

B. Fully-owned subsidiary   _1140/16 = 71.3%_

C. Autonomous division   _1360/20 = 68%_

D. Consolidated into existing units   _2050/30 = 68.4%_

E. Other (Please specify.) _____   _308/5 = 61.5%_

10. Was there a relatively typical pattern for the manner and extent of integration of the firms which were acquired during the concerned period?

Yes _23_   No _27_

If no, please skip to number 12.

11. Regarding this typical pattern, which of the following functions were consolidated? (Please indicate the approximate chronological order unless consolidation was simultaneous.)

A. Financial and accounting   _89 *_

B. Personnel and industrial relations   _69_

C. Legal   _83_

D. Purchasing   _38_

E. Sales promotion and advertising   _56_

F. Other marketing and distribution   _32_

G. Production, manufacturing   _38_

H. Research and development   _38_

I. Other (Please specify.) _____   _0_

Eight-point scale by chronological order

12. About how long did it take to integrate the operations of acquired firms? (Please indicate the proportion of firms in each category.)

A. Less than six months   *1510/19 = 79.5%*

B. Between six months and one year   *840/12 = 70%*

C. Between one and two years   *1248/16 = 78%*

D. More than two years   *1000/14 = 71.5%*

13. Was there generally an explicit forecast of post-acquisitions performance for an acquired firm?

   Yes *21 (S)* / *41 (M)*   No *13 (S)* / *7 (M)*

14. Since the concerned acquisition period, in general, how have the acquired firms compared to expectations on the following measure? (Please indicate the proportion of firms in each category if there was too great a variability to aggregate them meaningfully.

A. Profits:

   Higher *1350/18*   Lower *2100/27*   Same *1450/19*

B. Sales:

   Higher *1740/21*   Lower *1630/22*   Same *1185/18*

C. Profit Margins:

   Higher *1355/17*   Lower *1800/23*   Same *1350/17*

D. Other (Please specify): _____

   Higher *200/2*   Lower _____   Same _____

15. Would you please provide approximate figures for the following financial statistics of the acquired firms for the year preceding their acquisition.

Firm	Total Net Sales	Total Assets	Total Before Tax Earnings

Appendix B
SAMPLE COMPUTER PRINTOUT

FIRMS WITH ACCEPTABLE MERGER PROGRAMS

LOW GROWTH FIRMS

Performance Variables	(1) Pre-Acquisition Average Growth Rate	(2) Actual Post-Acquisition Average Growth Rate	(3) Difference Pre-Post Acquisition (2) - (1)	Total Period Average Growth Rate	Value Test Statistic For Significance	Mean Initial Year of Program NT0	Mean Year Prior to Acquisition NT1-1	Mean Last Year of Program NT 3
Sales Growth I	.88	9.01	8.13 1	5.44	8.50	.00	.00	.00
Earnings Growth I	3.78	26.14	22.36 1	16.46	4.30	.00	.00	.00
Earnings/Share Growth I	3.54	23.66	20.12 1	14.95	3.97	.00	.00	.00
Total Assets Growth I	2.82	7.34	4.52 1	5.71	5.30	.00	.00	.00
Earnings/Common Equity Growth I	-.80	19.00	19.81 1	9.47	3.98	.00	.00	.00
Sales Growth II	-.16	11.45	7.87 1	5.50	6.49	220.37	222.50	351.59
Earnings Growth II	-4.32	25.38	26.13 1	4.30	4.59	11.79	12.66	21.73
Earnings/Share Growth II	-4.51	18.31	24.81 1	2.78	4.56	2.12	1.45	2.16
Total Assets Growth II	3.97	9.00	1.58 1	7.07	1.80	128.44	162.61	249.69
Earnings/Common Equity Growth II	-7.93	11.68	24.70 1	-1.49	4.37	.16	.09	.12
Dividend/Earnings Growth II	10.55	.18	-7.66 1	2.72	-1.98	.57	.61	.49
Total Equity Growth II	5.67	6.87	-.78 0	6.94	-.91	84.83	109.70	155.66
Earnings/Total Assets Growth II	-7.50	14.79	22.13 1	-1.37	4.51	.13	.07	.09
Employees Growth II	-1.14	3.79	2.02 0	1.31	1.26	11.51	10.63	12.99
Stock Price Growth II	3.92	15.98	9.41 1	10.07	2.77	15.71	18.16	26.50
Total Debt/Equity Growth II	-2.84	5.98	6.22 1	1.11	3.23	.51	.41	.53
Earnings/Employee Growth II	7.17	13.52	5.94 0	6.36	1.14	101.50	1701.85	5051.15
Price/Earnings Ratio III	8.61	8.07	-.54 0	8.40	-1.22	.00	.00	.00
Total Debt/Equity Ratio III	.47	.51	.04 0	.49	1.12	.00	.00	.00
Payout Ratio III	.60	.52	-.08 1	.57	-2.06	.00	.00	.00
Price/Equity Ratio III	.61	.90	.29 1	.76	4.70	.00	.00	.00
Total Assets III	142.66	209.24	66.58 1	178.52	2.16	.00	.00	.00
Earnings/Common Equity Ratio III	.12	.10	-.02 1	.11	-4.13	.00	.00	.00

Appendix C

SAMPLE COMPUTER PROGRAM

```
C DIMENSIONING STATEMENTS
  DIMENSION  VARAVT (30,3,4)
  DIMENSION ADENOM(20), BDENOM(20). CDENOM(20), DDENOM(2)
  DIMENSION AASUM(20), BBSUM(20), CCSUM(20), DDSUM(20)
  DIMENSION SCCT(4,30), DEVT(4,30)
  DIMENSION M(20),VAR(20,20),VARGR(20,20),AVGR1(5),AVGR2(5)
  DIMENSION AVGR3(5),DATA(60,20)
  DIMENSION AVAR1(6),AVAR2(6),AVAR3(6)
  DIMENSION STKI(20),STK2(20),ISTK(20),STKD(20)
  DIMENSION STK(20),AVAR(6,20)
  DIMENSION STK3(20),STK4(20),DSTK(20)
  DIMENSION JSTK(20),STKE(20),ESTK(20)
  DIMENSION STKHI(20),STKLO(20)
  DIMENSION DJ(19)
  DIMENSION ASUM(5),BSUM(5),GSUM(5)
  DIMENSION DSUM(6),ESUM(6),FSUM(6)
  DIMENSION C(15),D(15),E(15),F(15)
  DIMENSION GSUM(5),HSUM(6)
  DIMENSION AVGR4(5),AVAR4(6)
  DIMENSION S(3,4,30),STD(3,4,30)
  DIMENSION SAA(4,70),SBB(4,70),SCC(4,70),SDEV(4,70)
  DIMENSION A(257),IA(257),B(1285)
  DIMENSION AV(4,30),XBAR(4,70)
  DIMENSION T(70),TVAR(4,30),TDEV(4,30)
  DIMENSION NSIG(100),U(100)
  DIMENSION SUM(15,3,4)
  DIMENSION VARAVG(30,4,4)
  REAL NT(4,20)
  DIMENSION YAVG(4,12,20)
  EQUIVALENCE (IA,A)
  INDIC=1
C SELECTION OPTIONS:  WILL POINT OUT RESULTS FOR EACH INDIVIDUAL FIRM OR BY GROWTH
1   CLASS
F INDIC=0 PRINT CALCULATIONS FOR EACH FIRM
F INDIC=1 PRINT ONLY SUMMARIES AT END
  ITS=0
F ITS=0 CALCULATIONS ON MERGER PROGS FROM SELECTED DATA CARDS
F ITS=1 CALCULATIONS FOR ALL FIRMS ON TAPE
F ITS=2 CALCULATIONS FOR ALL FIRMS WITH NO ACQUISITIONS
  IRW=0
F IRW=0 PROGRAM WILL REWIND TAPE 2 MORE TIMES MAKING TOTAL OF 3 RUNS
F IRW=1 PROGRAM WILL REWIND TAPE ONE TIME
F IRW=2 PROGRAM WILL ONLY RUN ONE TIME
C VARIABLE INITIALIZING STATEMENTS
  DO 47 K=1,19
46 FORMAT(F4,3)
  READ(5,46)(DJ(K))
47 CONTINUE
48 CONTINUE
  DO 49 L=1,70
```

```
        DO 49 J=1,4
        SBB(J,L)=0.
     49 CONTINUE
        DO50 I=1,3
        DO50 J=1,4
        DO50 K=1,30
        S(I,J,K)=0.
     50 CONTINUE
        DO 412 I=1,4
        DO 412 K=1,19
    412 NT(I,K)=0.
        DO 413 I=1,4
        DO 413 J=1,12
        DO 413 K=1,20
    413 YAVG(I,J,K)=0.
        DO 33K=1,15
        DO 33 J=1,3
        DO 33 L=1,4
     33 SUM(K,J,L)=0.
        TOT1=0.
        TOT2=0.
        TOT3=0.
        REWIND 4
     52 FORMAT(21H TAPE REWIND COMPLETE)
        WRITE(6,730)
        WRITE(6,52)
        JI=0
     99 IF(ITS-1)2,5,2
      C READS ACQUISITION DATA FROM CARDS
READ CARD
      1 FORMAT(2X,1912,9X,14,6X,16)
      2 READ(5,1)(M(I),I=1,19),151C,IFIRM
    801 FORMAT(5X,2110)
        WRITE(6,1801) ISIC,IFIRM
        IF(M(1)-99)4,990,4
      4 CONTINUE
      5 CONTINUE
      C READS COMPUSTAT FINANCIAL DATA
READ 5 TAPE RECORDS AND ASSEMBLE INTO DATA RECORD
        NWORD=257
        DO 15 KN=1,5
        CALL NTRAN(4,2,NWORD,A,L)
      6 IF(L+1)20,6,11
NTRAN ERROR CODES
L= -1 TRANSMISSION NOT COMPLETE
L= -2 END OF FILE
L= -3 DEVICE ERROR
L= -4 TRANSMISSION ABORT
     11 DO 13 IW=1,NWORD
        IF(A(IW))12,13,13
     12 IA(IW)=-FLD(1,35,IA(IW))
```

```
 13 CONTINUE
    IF(KN-1)72,71,72
 71 DO 171 J=1,255
171 B(J)=A(J)
    GO TO 80
 72 IF(KN-2)74,73,74
 73 DO 173 J=1,255
173 B(J+255)=A(J)
    TO TO 80
 74 IF(KN-3)76,75,76
 75 DO 175 J=1,255
175 B(J+510)=A(J)
    GO TO 80
 76 IF(KN-4)78,77,78
 77 DO 177 J=1,255
177 B(J+765)=A(J)
    GO TO 80
 78 IF(KN-5)80,79,80
 79 DO 179 J=1,255
179 B(J+1020)=A(J)
 80 CONTINUE
 15 CONTINUE
    DO 96 J=2,1270
 96 B(J-1)=B(J)
    JSIC=B(1201)
    JFIRM=B(1202)
    JK=0
    DO 90 J=1,20
    DO 90 I=1,60
    JK=JK+1
    DATA(I,J)=B(JK)
 90 CONTINUE
    IF(ITS-1)97,317,91
 91 IF(ITS-2)2,92,2
 92 IF(JFIRM-IFIRM)5,317,5
 97 CONTINUE
    IF(IFIRM-JFIRM)5,16,5
 16 CONTINUE
  C SELECTION OF ACCEPTABLE ACQUISITION PERIOD:  (1) AT LEAST 4 YEARS PRIOR TO ANY
  1 ACQUISITION  (2) AT LEAST 2 YEARS AFTER LAST ACQUISITION  (3) NO MORE THAN ONE
  1 YEAR IN SUCCESSION WITHOUT ACQUISITION
    N2=4
    N=2
    K=0
    DO100 I=1,19
    IR=20-1
    IR(M(IR))30,45,30
 45 K=K+1
    GO TO 100
 30 IF(K-N)51,110,110
 51 K=0
    GO TO 100
110 L=0
    MTOT=0
```

```
      NT2=21-1
      NT3=NT2+K-1
      00 300 J=1,19
      JR=20-J
      IF(M(JR))130,120,130
  120 L=L+1
      GO TO 300
  130 IF(L-N2)150,140,140
  140 NTO=JR+1
      NT1=NTO+L
      GO TO 897
  150 IF(L-1)170,170,160
  160 IR=J-L
      GO TO 51
  170 MTOT=MTOT+M(JR)
      L=0
  300 CONTINUE
      IF(L-N2)2,310,310
  100 CONTINUE
      GO TO 2
  310 NTO=1
      NT1=L+1
  397 MSUM=0.
      DO 899 I=NTO,NT3
    C COUNTER ON NUMBER OF ACQUISITIONS
  399 MSUM=MSUM+M(I)
      GO TO 318
    C ARBITRARY ACQUISITION PROGRAM FOR NONMERGING FIRMS
  317 NTO=1
      NT2=14
      NT1=7
      NT3=19
    C DATA CHECK FOR ABSENCE OF DATA
  318 IF(DATA(8,NTO)-.01)350,350,320
  320 IF(DATA(11,NTO)-.01)350,350,322
  322 IF(DATA(12,NTO)-.01)350,350,324
  324 IF(DATA(18,NTO)-.01)350,350,326
  326 IF(DATA(21,NTO)-.01)350,350,328
  328 IF(DATA(22,NTO)-.01)350,350,330
  330 IF(DATA(23,NTO)-.01)350,350,332
  332 IF(DATA(25,NTO)-.01)350,350,334
  334 IF(DATA(29,NTO)-.01)350,350,336
  336 IF(DATA( 6,NTO)-.01)350,350,391
  350 NTO=NTO+1
      NNTO=NT1-NTO
      IF(NNTO-4)360,318,318
  360 IF(ITS-1)2,5,2
  391 NA=NT1-1
      NB=NTO+1
      NC=NT3-NT1+1
      ND=NT3-NT2+1
      NE=NT1-NTO
      NF=NA-NTO
      ANC=NC
      BND=ND
      ANE=NE
```

```
      ANF=NF
      ERNSM=0.
CALCULATE PERFORMANCE VARIABLES
DATA(27,J) IS SHARE ADJUSTMENT FACTOR
    C SMOOTHING FUNCTION ON PER SHARE EARNINGS TO ADJUST VIOLENT FLUCTUATIONS
      DO 451 J=1,19
  451 ERNSM=ERNSM+DATA(18,J)
      AVERN=ERNSM/19.
      PEREN=.2*AVERN
      NT4=NTO+1
      DO 69 J=NT4,NT3
      IF(DATA(18,J)-PEREN/2.)65,65,69
   65 DATA(18,J)=DATA(18,J-1)+DATA(18,J)+DATA(18,J+1)
      DATA(18,J)=DATA(18,J)/3.
      IF(DATA(18,J)-PEREN/2.)350,350,69
   69 CONTINUE
      DO453 J=6,12,6
      DATSUM=0.
      DO 452 I=NTO,19
  452 DATSUM=DATSUM+DATA(J,I)
      DIV=19-NTO+1
      ADATM=DATSUM/DIV*,1
      DO 453 I=NB,NT3
      IF(DATA(J,I)-ADATM)454,454,453
  454 DATA(J,I=(DATA(J,I-1)+DATA(J,I)+DATA(J,I+1))/3.
  453 CONTINUE
    C VARIABLE ASSIGNMENTS
      DO 450 J=1,19
      VAR(1,J)=DATA(12,J)
      VAR(2,J)=DATA(18,J)
      VAR(3,J)=1000.*(DATA(18,J)/(DATA(25,J)*DATA(27,J)))
      VAR(4,J)=DATA(6,J)
      VAR(5,J)=DATA(18,J)/DATA(11,J)
      VAR(6,J)=DATA(21,J)/DATA(18,J)
      VAR(7,J)=DATA(10,J)+DATA(11,J)
      VAR(8,J)=DATA(18,J)/(DATA(9,J)+DATA(10,J)+DATA(11,J))
      VAR(9,J)=DATA( 29,J)
      VAR(11,J)=(DATA(5,J)+DATA(9,J))/(DATA(6,J)-DATA(5,J)-DATA(9,J))
      VAR(12,J)=DATA(18,J)/DATA(29,J)
  450 CONTINUE
    C CALCULATION OF AVERAGE STOCK PRICE ADJUSTED FOR ALL SPLITS, DIVIDENDS, ETC. AND
    1 FOR DOW-JONES AVERAGE MOVEMENT
      DO 500 J=1,19
      STK1(J)=DATA(22,J)
      ISTK(J)=STK1(J)
      STK2(J)=ISTK(J)
      STKD(J)=(STK1(J)-STK2(J))*10.
      DSTK(J)=STKD(J)*0.125
      STKHI(J)=STK2(J)+DSTK(J)
      STK3(J)=DATA(23,J)
      JSTK(J)=STK3(J)
```

    NOTE: DATA VARIABLES 9 AND 12 CONTAINED NUMEROUS ERRORS AND THUS THESE
            VARIABLES WERE DELETED FROM THE STUDY.

```
      STK4(J)=JSTK(J)
      STKE(J)=(STK3(J)-STK4(J))*10.
      ESTK(J)=STKE(J)*0.125
      STKLO(J)=STK4(J)+ESTK(J)
      STK(J)=0.5*(STKHI(J)+STKLO(J))
      VAR(10,J)=STK(J)/DATA(27,J)
      AVAR(1,J)=.001*(STK(J)*DATA(25,J)/(DATA(18,J)*DJ(J)))
      IF(AVAR(1,J))496,496,497
496   AVAR(1,J)=0.
497   CONTINUE
    C CLASS III VARIABLE CALCULATIONS
      AVAR( 2,J)=(DATA(9,J)+DATA(S,J))/(DATA(6,J)-DATA(9,J)-DATA(5,J))
      AVAR(3,J)=DATA(21,J)/DATA(18,J)
      IF(AVAR(3,J))498,498,499
498   AVAR(3,J)=0.
499   CONTINUE
      AVAR(4,J)=.001*(DATA(25,J)*STK(J)/(DATA(11,J)*DATA(27,J)))
      AVAR(5,J)=VAR(4,J)
      AVAR(6,J)=VAR(5,J)
500   CONTINUE
    C CALCULATION OF CLASS I VARIABLES
      DO600 I=1,5
      ASUM(1)=0,0
      DO 502 J=NB,19
502   VARGR(I,J)=(VAR(I,J)-VAR(I,J-1))/VAR(I,J-1)
      IF(NTO-1)530,510,530
510   DO 520 J=NB,NA
      ASUM(I)=ASUM(I)+VARGR(I,J)
520   CONTINUE
      NUMBR=NT1-NTO-1
      DIV=NUMBR
      AVGR1(I)=100.*(ASUM(I)/DIV)
      GO TO 550
530   DO540 J=NB,NA
      ASUM(I)=ASUM(I)+VARGR(I,J)
540   CONTINUE
      NUMBER=NT1-NTO-1
      DIV=NUMBR
      AVGR1(I)=100.*(ASUM(I)/DIV)
550   CONTINUE
      BSUM(I)=0.
      DO560 J=NT1,NT3
      BSUM(I)=BSUM(I)+VARGR(I,J)
560   CONTINUE
      NUMBR=NT3-NT1+1
      DIV=NUMBR
      AVGR3(I)=100.*(BSUM(I)/DIV)
      CSUM(I)=0.
      DO 570 J=NT2,NT3
      CSUM(I)=CSUM(I)+VARGR(I,J)
570   CONTINUE
      NUMBR=NT3-NT2+1
      DIV=NUMBR
      AVGR2(1)=100.*(CSUM(I)/DIV)
      GSUM(I)=0.
```

```
      DO 580 J=NB,NT3
      GSUM(I)=GSUM(I)+VARGR(I,J)
  580 CONTINUE
      NUMBR=NT3-NT0
      DIV=NUMBR
      AVGR4(I)=100.*(GSUM(I)/DIV)
      T(I)=AVGR3(I)-AVGR1(I)
  600 CONTINUE
    C CALCULATION OF CLASS III VARIABLES
      DO 650 I=1,6
      DSUM(I)=0.
      DO610 J=NOT,NA
      DSUM(I)=DSUM(I)+AVAR(I,J)
  610 CONTINUE
      NUMBR=NT1-NTO
      DIV=NUMBR
      AVAR1(I)=DSUM(I)/DIV
      ESUM(I)=0.
      DO620 J=NT1,NT3
      ESUM(I)=ESUM(I)+AVAR(I,J)
  620 CONTINUE
      NUMBR=NT3-NT1+1
      DIV=NUMBR
      AVAR3(I)=ESUM(I)/DIV
      FSUM(I)=0.
      DO630 J=NT2,NT3
      FSUM(I)=FSUM(I)+AVAR(I,J)
  630 CONTINUE
      NUMBR=NT3-NT2+1
      DIV=NUMBR
      AVAR2(I)=FSUM(I)/DIV
      HSUM(I)=0.
      DO 640 J=NTO,NT3
      HSUM(I)=HSUM(I)+AVAR(I,J)
  640 CONTINUE
      NUMBR=NT3-NTO+1
      DIV=NUMBR
      AVAR4(I)=HSUM(I)/DIV
      T(I+17)=AVAR3(I)-AVAR1(I)
  650 CONTINUE
    C CALCULATION OF CLASS II VARIABLES
      DO 167 I=1,12
      AASUM(I)=0.
      BBSUM(I)=0.
      CCSUM(I)=0.
      DO 161 J=NTO,NA
  161 AASUM(I)=AASUM(I)+VAR(I,J)
      DO 162 J=NT1,NT3
  162 BBSUM(I)=BBSUM(I)+VAR(I,J)
      DDSUM(I)=AASUM(I)+BBSUM(I)
      NT5=NT2-1
      DO 163 J=NT5,NT3
  163 CCSUM(I)=CCSUM(I)+VAR(I,J)
      DIV=NA-NTO+1
```

```
      ADENOM(I)=AASUM(I)/DIV
      DIV=NT3-NA
      BDENOM(I)=BBSUM(I)/DIV
      DIV=NT3-NTO+1
      DDENOM(I)=DDSUM(I)/DIV
      DIV=NT3-NT2+1
      CDENOM(I)=CCSUM(I)/DIV
  167 CONTINUE
    C AVERAGE VALUES OF PERFORMANCE VARIABLES FOR FIRST AND LAST YEARS AND LAST YEAR
    1 FOR ACQUISITION PROGRAM
      DO 119 I=1,12
      IF(VAR(I,NTO)-ADENOM(I)*.1)111,111,112
  111 VAR(I,NTO)=ADENOM(I)
  112 IF(VAR(I,NA)-.1*BDENOM(I))113,113,114
  113 VAR(I,NA)=BDENOM(I)
  114 IF(VAR(I,NT2-1)-.1*CDENOM(I))115,115,119
  115 VAR(I,NT2-1)=CDENOM(I)
  119 CONTINUE
      IF(VAR(12,NTO)-.1*ADENOM(12))121,121,122
  121 VAR(12,NTO)=(VAR(12,NB)+VAR(12,NTO+2))/2.
  122 CONTINUE
      DO 660 I=1,12
      IF(VAR(I,NTO)-.01)651,651,652
  651 C(I)=0.
      D(I)=0.
      E(I)=0.
      F(I)=0.
      GO TO 660
    C CLASS II VARIABLES
  652 AAA=NA-NTO
      BBB=NT3-NT1+1
      CCC=NT3-NT2+1
      DDD=NT3-NTO+1
      C(I)=100.*(VAR(I,NA)-VAR(I,NTO))/(VAR(I,NTO)+AAA)
      D(I)=100.*(VAR(I,NT3)-VAR(I,NT2-1))/(VAR(I,NT2-1)*CCC)
      E(I)=100.*(VAR(I,NT3)-VAR(I,NA))/(VAR(I,NA)*868)
      F(I)=100.*(VAR(I,NT3)-VAR(I,NTO))/(VAR(I,NTO)*000)
  660 CONTINUE
    C UPPER BOUND ON GROWTH RATE (CLASS II) OF 100%
      IF(C(12).GT.100.)C(12)=100.
      IF(D(12).GT.100.)D(12)=100.
      IF(E(12).GT.100.(E(12)=100.
      IF(F(12).GT.100.)F(12)=100.
    C TRANSFER TO INDIVIDUAL OR SUMMARY CALCULATIONS
      DO 661 I=1,12
  661 T(I+5)=D(I)-C(I)
      IF(INDIC-1)671,800,671
  671 CONTINUE
    C INDIVIDUAL FIRM ACQUISITION PROGRAM PERFORMANCE CALCULATION
      LA=NTO+1946
      LB=NT1+1946
      LC=NT2+1946
      LD=NT3+1946
```

```
    LX=LB
    LY=NT2+1945
900 FORMAT(1H1)
    WRITE(6,900)
902 FORMAT(33X,6H FIRM ,16,7X,4HSIC ,14)
    WRITE(6,902) IFIRM,ISIC
    IF(MTOT-1)1903,982,1903
803 CONTINUE
903 FORMAT(31X,20HMERGER PROGRAM FROM, I4,4H TO ,I4)
    WRITE(6,903) LX,LY
    GO TO 1905
981 FORMAT(34X,21HMERGER PROGRAM DURING,I5)
802 WRITE(6,981) LX
805 CONTINUE
905 FORMAT(35X,20H'TOTAL ACQUISITIONS .I3///)
906 FORMAT(45X,7H ACTUAL,7X,11H DIFFERENCE)
908 FORMAT(31X,5H PRE-,10X,6H POST-,8X,9H PRE-POST,10X,5HTOTAL)
910 FORMAT(27X,12H ACQUISITION,5X,11HACQUISITION,5X,11HACQUISITION,
   17X,6HPERIOD,5X,5HVALUE,5X,3HNTO,6X,5HNT1-1,5X,3HNT3//)
904 FORMAT(4X,42H AVERAGE OF ANNUAL PERCENTAGE GROWTH RATES/)
    WRITE(6,905) MTOT
    WRITE(6,906)
    WRITE(6,908)
    WRITE(6,910)
    WRITE(6,904)
912 FORMAT(6H SALES,20X,F9.2,3F16.2)
914 FORMAT(9H EARNINGS,17X,F9.2,3F16,2)
916 FORMAT(19H EARNINGS PER SHARE,4F16.2)
918 FORMAT(13H TOTAL ASSETS,6X,4F16.2)
920 FORMAT(19H EARNINGS TO EQUITY,4F16.2//)
    WRITE(6,912) AVGR1(1),AVGR3(1),T(1),AVGR4(1)
    WRITE(6,914) AVGR1(2),AVGR3(2),T(2),AVGR4(2)
    WRITE(6,916) AVGR1(3),AVGR3(3),T(3),AVGR4(3)
    WRITE(6,918) AVGR1(4),AVGR3(4),T(4),AVGR4(4)
    WRITE(6,920) AVGR1(5),AVGR3(5),T(5),AVGR4(5)
940 FORMAT(4X,43H AVERAGE PERCENTAGE GROWTH RATE OVER PERIOD/)
    WRITE(6,940)
942 FORMAT(6H SALES,13X,4F16.2)
944 FORMAT(9H EARNINGS,10X,4F16.2)
946 FORMAT (19H EARNINGS PER SHARE,4F16.2)
922 FORMAT(13H TOTAL ASSETS,6X,4F16.2)
921 FORMAT(14H  PAYOUT RATIO,5X,4F16.2)
922 FORMAT(14H COMMON EQUITY,5X,4F16.2)
923 FORMAT(19H EARN/TOTAL CAPITAL,4F16.2)
924 FORMAT(19H EARNINGS TO EQUITY,4F16.2)
925 FORMAT(16H TOTAL EMPLOYEES,3X,4F16.2)
926 FORMAT(18H STOCK PRICE (ADJ),1X,4F16.2)
927 FORMAT(18H TOTAL DEDT/EQUITY,1X,4F16.2)
928 FORMAT(18H EARNINGS/EMPLOYEE,1X,4F16.2//)
```

```
      WRITE(6,942) C(1),E(1),T(6),F(1)
       WRITE(6,944) C(2),E(2),T(7),F(2)
       WRITE(6,946) C(3),E(3),T(8),F(3)
       WRITE(6,922) C(4),E(4),T(9),F(4)
      WRITE(6,1921)C(6),E(6),T(11),F(6)
      WRITE(6,1922)C(7),E(7),T(12),F(7)
      WRITE(6,1923)C(8),E(8),T(13),F(8)
      WRITE(6,924) C(5),E(5),T(10),F(5)
      WRITE(6,925) C(9),E(9),T(14),F(9)
      WRITE(6,926)C(10),E(10),T(15),F(10)
      WRITE(6,927)C(11),E(11),T(16),F(11)
      WRITE(6,928)C(12),E(12),T(17),F(12)
  930 FORMAT(4X,15H AVERAGE VALUES/)
  932 FORMAT(19H P/E RATIO ADJUSTED,4F16.2)
  934 FORMAT(19H EARNINGS PER SHARE,4F16.2)
  936 FORMAT(22H DIVIDENDS TO EARNINGS,7X,F6.2,3F16.2)
  936 FORMAT(14H COMMON EQUITY,5X,4F16.2)
  937 FORMAT(19H EARN/TOTAL CAPITAL,4F16.2)
  938 FORMAT(19H PRICE EQUITY RATIO,4F16.2//)
      WRITE(6,930)
      WRITE(6,932) AVAR1(1),AVAR3(1),T(18),AVAR4(1)
      WRITE(6,934) AVAR1(2),AVAR3(2),T(19),AVAR4(2)
      WRITE(6,936) AVAR1(3),AVAR3(3),T(20),AVAR4(3)
      WRITE(6,1936)AVAR1(5),AVAR3(5),T(22),AVAR4(5)
      WRITE(6,1937)AVAR1(6),AVAR3(6),T(23),AVAR4(6)
      WRITE(6,938) AVAR1(4),AVAR3(4),T(21),AVAR4(4)
  960 FORMAT(4X,40H ABSOLUTE VALUES OF PERFORMANCE MEASURES/)
      WRITE(6,960)
  962 FORMAT(33X,I4,12X,I4,12X,I4,12X,I4/)
      WRITE(6,962)LA,LB,LC,LD
  972 FORMAT(13H SALES ($MIL),9X,4F16.2)
  974 FORMAT(16H EARNINGS ($MIL),6X,4F16.2)
  976 FORMAT(14H EQUITY ($MIL),8X,4F16.2)
  978 FORMAT(19H EARNINGS TO EQUITY,3X,4F16.2)
  979 FORMAT(22H AVERAGE STOCK PRICE ,4F16.2)
  980 FORMAT(22H P/E RATIO ADJUSTED   ,4F16.2//)
      WRITE(6,972) VAR(1,NTO,VAR(1,NT)),VAR(1,NT2),VAR(1,NT3)
      WRITE(6,974) VAR(2,NTO),VAR(2,NT1),VAR(2,NT2),VAR(2,NT3)
      WRITE(6,976) DATA(11,NTO),DATA(11,NT1),DATA(11,N12),DATA(11,NT3)
      WRITE(6,978) VAR(5,NTO),VAR(5,NT1),VAR(5,NT2),VAR(5,NT3)
      WRITE(6,979) STK(NTO),STK(NT1),STK(NT2),STK(NT3)
      WRITE(6,980) AVAR(1,NTO),AVAR(1,NT1),AVAR(1,NT2),AVAR(1,NT3)
  800 CONTINUE
    C SUMMARY PROGRAM BROKEN DOWN BY GROWTH CLASS
  800 FORMAT(2I10)
      WRITE(6,1800) JSIC,JFIRM
    C GROWTH CLASS CHECK
      IF(ITS)801,801,806
  801 IF(C(1)-4.)951,951,805
  805 IF(C(1)-10.)953,953,955
  806 IF(F(1)-4.)951,951,807
  807 IF(F(1)-10.)953,953,955
```

```
950 FORMAT(26H THIS IS A LOW GROWTH FIRM)
952 FORMAT(29H THIS IS A MEDIUM GROWTH FIRM)
954 FORMAT(27H THIS IS A HIGH GROWTH FIRM)
951 CONTINUE                       .
    IF(INDIC-1)1950,1951,1950
950 WRITE(6,950)
951 TOT1=TOT1+1.
    I=1
    DO 401 J=1,12
    DO 401 K=NTO,NT3
401 YAVG(I,J,K)=YAVG(I,J,K)+VAR(J,K)/VAR(J,NTO)
    DO 402 K=NTO,NT3
402 NT(I,K)=NT(I,K)+1.
    DO 27 L=1,12
    SUM(L,1,1)=SUM(L,1,1)+VAR(L,NTO)
    SUM(L,2,1)=SUM(L,2,1)+VAR(L,NT1-1)
 27 SUM(L,3,1)=SUM(L,3,1)+VAR(L,NT3)
    GO TO 700
953 CONTINUE
  C THE REMAINDER OF THIS PROGRAM SIMPLY AGGREGATES THE DATA, COMPUTES THE MEANS AND
  1 STANDARD DEVIATIONS OF PERFORMANCE MEASURES, AND TESTS FOR SIGNIFICANCE OF CHANGE
  1 IN PERFORMANCE
    IF(INDIC-1)1952,1953,1952
952 WRITE(6,952)
953 TOT2=TOT2+1.
    I=2
    DO 403 J=1,12
    DO 402 K=NTO,NT3
403 YAVG(I,J,K)=YAVG(I,J,K)+VAR(J,K)/VAR(J,NTO)
    DO 404 K=NTO,NT3
404 NT(I,K)=NT(I,K)+1.
    DO 28 L=1,12
    SUM(L,1,2)=SUM(L,1,2)+VAR(L,NTO)
    SUM(L,2,2)=SUM(L,2,2)+VAR(L,NT1-1)
 28 SUM(L,3,2)=SUM(L,3,2)+VAR(L,NT3)
    GO TO 700
955 CONTINUE
    IF(INDIC-1)1954,1955,1954
954 WRITE(6,954)
955 TOT3=TOT3+1.
    I=3
    DO 405 J=1,12
    DO 405 K=NTO,NT3
405 YAVG(I,J,K)=YAVG(I,J,K)+VAR(J,K)/VAR(J,NTO)
    DO 406 K=NTO,NT3
406 NT(I,K)=NT(I,K)+1.
    DO 29 L=1,12
    SUM(L,1,3)=SUM(L,1,3)+VAR(L,NTO)
    SUM(L,2,3)=SUM(L,2,3)+VAR(L,NT1-1)
 29 SUM(L,3,3)=SUM(L,3,3)+VAR(L,NT3)
700 CONTINUE
    DO 32 L=1,12
```

```fortran
      SUM(L,1,4)=SUM(L,1,4)+VAR(L,NTO)
      SUM(L,2,4)=SUM(L,2,4)+VAR(L,NT1-1)
   32 SUM(L,3,4)=SUM(L,3,4)+VAR(L,NT3)
      DO701 K=1,5
      S(I,1,K)=S(I,1,K)+AVGR1(K)
      S(I,2,K)=S(I,2,K)+AVGR3(K)
      S(I,3,K)=S(I,3,K)+T(K)
      S(I,4,K)=S(I,4,K)+AVGR4(K)
      IF(I-1)1700,1700,1701
  700 KA=K
      GO TO 1704
  701 IF(I-2)1702,1702,1703
  702 KA=K+23
      GO TO 1704
  703 KA=K+46
  704 CONTINUE
      SAA(1,KA)=(AVGR1(K))**2.
      SAA(2,KA)=(AVGR3(K))**2.
      SAA(3,KA)=(T(K))**2.
      SAA(4,KA)=(AVGR4(K))**2.
      DO 1705 L=1,4
  705 SBB(K,KA)=SBB(L,KA)+SAA(L,KA)
  701 CONTINUE
      DO 702 K=18,23
      KK=K-17
      S(I,1,K)=S(I,1,K)+AVAR1(KK)
      S(I,2,K)=S(I,2,K)+AVAR3(KK)
      S(I,3,K)=S(I,3,K)+T(K)
      S(I,4,K)=S(I,4,K)+AVAR4(KK)
      IF(I-1)1711,1711,1712
  711 KA=K
      GO TO 1715
  712 IF(I-2)1713,1713,1714
  713 KA=K+23
      GO TO 1715
  714 KA=K+46
  715 CONTINUE
      SAA(1,KA)=(AVAR1(KK))**2.
      SAA(2,KA)=AVAR3(KK))**2.
      SAA(3,KA)=(T(K))**2.
      SAA(4,KA)=(AVAR4(KK))**2.
      DO 1716 L=1,4
  716 SBB(K,KA)=SBB(L,KA)+SAA(L,KA)
  702 CONTINUE
      DO 703 K=6,17
      KKK=K-5
      S(I,1,K)=S(I,1,K)+C(KKK)
      S(I,2,K)=S(I,2,K)+E(KKK)
      S(I,3,K)=S(I,3,K)+T(K)
      S(I,4,K)=S(I,4,K)+F(KKK)
      IF(I-1)1721,1721,1722
  721 KA=K
      GO TO 1725
```

```
722 IF(I-2)1723,1723,1724
723 KA=K+23
    GO TO 1725
724 KA=K+46
725 CONTINUE
    SAA(1,KA)=(C(KKK))**2.
    SAA(2,KA)=(E(KKK))**2.
    SAA(3,KA)=(T(K))**2.
    SAA(4,KA)=(F(KKK))**2.
    DO 1726 L=1,4
726 SBB(L,KA)=SBB(L,KA)+SAA(L,KA)
703 CONTINUE
    IF(ITS-1)2,5,2
990 CONTINUE
    ITS=0
    DO 407 J=1,12
    DO 407 K=1,19
407 YAVG(4,J,K)=YAVG(1,J,K)+YAVG(2,J,K)+YAVG(3,J,K)
    DO 411 K=1,19
411 NT(4,K)=NT(1,K)+NT(2,K)+NT(3,K)
    DO 408I=1,4
    DO 408 J=1,12
    DO 408 K=1,19
408 YAVG(I,J,K)=YAVG(I,J,K)/NT(I,K)
    DO 410 I=1,4
    DO 410 J=1,12
410 WRITE(6,409) (I,J,K,(YAVG(I,J,K),K=1,19))
409 FORMAT(1X,3I4,10F10.3/13X,9F10.3,//)
    TOT4=TOT1+TOT2+TOT3
    DO 720 J=1,4
    DO 719 K=1,23
    STD(1,J,K)=S(1,J,K)/TOT1
    STD(2,J,K)=S(2,J,K)/TOT2
    STD(3,J,K)=S(3,J,K)/TOT3
    AV(J,K)=(S(1,J,K)+S(2,J,K)+S(3,J,K))/TOT4
719 CONTINUE
    DO720 L=1,69
    IF(L-23)711,711,712
711 TT=TOT1
    XBAR(J,L)=STD(1,J,L)
    GO TO 715
712 IF(L-46)713,713,714
713 TT=TOT2
    XBAR(J,L)=STD(2,J,L-23)
    GO TO 715
714 TT=TOT3
    XBAR(J,L)=STD(3,J,L-46)
715 CONTINUE
    SCC(J,L)=SBB(J,L)/TT-(XBAR(J,L))**2.
    SDEV(J,L)=SQRT(SCC(J,L))
720 CONTINUE
    DO 34 I=1,12
    DO 34 K=1,3
 34 VARAVG(I,K,1)=SUM(I,K,1)/TOT1
```

```
    DO 35 I=1,12
    DO 35 K=1,3
 35 VARAVG(I,K,2)=SUM(I,K,2)/TOT2
    DO 36 I=1,12
    DO 36 K=1,3
 36 VARAVG(I,K,3)=SUM(I,K,3)/TOT3
    DO 37 I=1,12
    DO 37 K=1,3
 37 VARAVG(I,K,4)=SUM(I,K,4)/TOT4
    DO 42 K=1,12
    DO 42 J=1,3
    DO 42 L=1,4
 42 VARAVT(K+5,J,L)=VARAVG(K,J,L)
    DO 38 K=1,5
    DO 38 J=1,3
    DO 38 L=1,4
 38 VARAVT(K,J,L)=0.
    DO 39 K=18,23
    DO 39 J=1,3
     DO 39 L=1,4
 39 VARAVT(K,J,L)=0.
    CALCULATIONS FOR THE TOTAL SAMPLE
    DO 729 L=1,23
    DO 729 J=1,4
    SCCT(J,L)=(SBB(J,L)+SBB(J,L+23)+SBB(J,L+46))/TOT4 -AV(J,L)**2
729 SDEVT(J,L)=SQRT(SCCT(J,L))
730 FORMAT(1H1)
    STOT1=SQRT(TOT1)
    STOT2=SQRT(TOT2)
    STOT3=SQRT(TOT3)
    STOT4=SQRT(TOT4)
    T1=(TOT1/TOT4)**2.
    T2=(TOT2/TOT4)**2.
    T3=(TOT3/TOT4)**2.
    DO 780 K=1,92
    IF(K-23)781,781,782
781 U(K)=XBAR(3,K)*STOT1/SDEV(3,K)
    GO TO 785
782 IF(K-46)783,783,784
783 U(K)=XBAR(3,K)*STOT2/SDEV(3,K)
    GO TO 785
784 IF(K-69)787,787,788
787 U(K)=XBAR(3,K)*STOT3/SDEV(3,K)
    GO TO 785
788 U(K)=AV(3,K-69)*STOT4/SDEVT(3,K-69)
785 CONTINUE
    IF(U(K)-1.65)789,786,786
789 IF(1.65+U(K))786,786,780
786 NSIG(K)=1
780 CONTINUE
     DO 790 I=1,4
    DO 790 J=1,23
    TVAR(I,J)=T1*SCC(I,J)+T2*SCC(I,J+23)+T3*SCC(I,J+46)
```

```
      TDEV(I,J)=SQRT(TVAR(I,J))
  790 CONTINUE
      WRITE(6,730)
  754 FORMAT(25X,38H FIRMS WITH ACCEPTABLE MERGER PROGRAMS/)
  758 FORMAT(25X,27H FIRMS WITH NO ACQUISITIONS/)
  759 FORMAT(25X,28H ALL FIRMS ON COMPUSTAT TAPE/)
      IF(ITS)1731,1730,1731
  730 WRITE(6,754)
      GO TO 1734
  731 IF(ITS-1)1733,1732,1733
  732 WRITE(6,759)
      GO TO 1734
  733 WRITE(6,758)
  734 CONTINUE
  732 FORMAT(34H AVERAGES OF PERFORMANCE VARIABLES//)
      WRITE(6,732)
      WRITE(6,906)
      WRITE(6,908)
      WRITE(6,910)
  733 FORMAT(/)
  734 FORMAT(11H LOW GROWTH)
      WRITE(6,734)
  736 FORMAT(19X,4F16.2)
  737 FORMAT(67X,F16.2,10X,3F9.2)
  707 FORMAT(67X,F16.2)
  739 FORMAT(19X,3F16.2,12,F14.2,F10.2,3F9.2)
      IF(ITS)771,770,771
  770 CONTINUE
      DO 1770 K=1,23
      WRITE(6,739) STD(1,1,K),STD(1,2,K),STD(1,3,K),NSIG(K),STD(1,4,K),0
     1(K),VARAVT(K,1,1),VARAVT(K,2,1),VARAVT(K,3,1)
  770 CONTINUE
      GO TO 772
  771 DO 1771 K=1,23
  771 WRITE(6,737) STD(1,4,K),          VARAVT(K,1,1),VARAVT(K,2,1),VARAVT
     1(K,3,1)
  772 CONTINUE
      WRITE(6,733)
  738 FORMAT(14H MEDIUM GROWTH)
      WRITE(6,738)
      IF(ITS)774,773,774
  773 CONTINUE
      DO 1773 K=1,23
      KU=K+23
      WRITE(6,739)STD(2,1,K),STD(2,2,K),STD(2,3,K),NSIG(KU),STD(2,4,K),U
     1(KU),VARAVT(K,1,2),VARAVT(K,2,2),VARAVT(K,3,2)
 1773 CONTINUE
      GO TO 775
  774 DO 1774 K=1,23
 1774 WRITE(6,737) STD(2,4,K),          VARAVT(K,1,2),VARAVT(K,2,2),VARAVT
     1(K,3,2)
  775 CONTINUE
      WRITE(6,733)
  740 FORMAT(12H HIGH GROWTH)
      WRITE(6,740)
      IF(ITS)777,776,777
```

141

```
 776 CONTINUE
     DO 1776 K=1,23
     KT=K+46
     WRITE(6,739)STD(3,1,K),STD(3,2,K),STD(3,3,K),NSIG(KT),STD(3,4,K),U
    1(KT),VARAVT(K,1,3),VARAVT(K, 2,3),VARAVT(K,3,3)
1776 CONTINUE
     GO TO 778
 777 DO 1777 K=1,23
1777 WRITE(6,737) STD(3,4,K),          VARAVT(K,1,3),VARAVT(K,2,3),VARAVT
    1(K,3,3)
 778 CONTINUE
     MTOT1=TOT1
     MTOT2=TOT2
     MTOT3=TOT3
     MTOT4=TOT4
 750 FORMAT(15,20H FIRMS IN LOW GROWTH)
 751 FORMAT(15,23H FIRMS IN MEDIUM GROWTH)
 752 FORMAT(15,21H FIRMS IN HIGH GROWTH)
 753 FORMAT(15,12H FIRMS TOTAL)
 721 FORMAT(41H 1 FOLLOWING NUMBER IN DIFFERENCE COLUMN ,
    148HINDICATES DIFFERENCE IS SIGNIFICANTLY DIFFERENT ,
    229HFROM ZERO AT 5 PER CENT LEVEL)
     WRITE(6,733)
     WRITE(6,750) MTOT1
     WRITE(6,751) MTOT2
     WRITE(6,752) MTOT3
     WRITE(6,753) MTOT4
     IF(ITS)1756,1755,1756
1755 WRITE(6,733)
     WRITE(6,721)
     WRITE(6,733)
1756 CONTINUE
     WRITE(6,730)
     IF(ITS)1761,1760,1761
1760 WRITE(6,754)
     GO TO 1764
1761 IF(ITS-1)1763,1762,1763
1762 WRITE(6,759)
     GO TO 1764
1763 WRITE(6,758)
1764 CONTINUE
 760 FORMAT(45H STANDARD DEVIATIONS OF PERFORMANCE VARIABLES//)
     WRITE(6,760)
     WRITE(6,906)
     WRITE(6,908)
     WRITE(6,910)
     WRITE(6,734)
     IF(ITS)792,791,792
 791 WRITE(6,736)((SDEV(L,KA),L=1,4),KA=1,23)
     GO TO 793
 792 WRITE(6,707)(SDEV(4,KA),KA=1,23)
 793 CONTINUE
     WRITE(6,733)
```

```
      WRITE(6,738)
      IF(ITS)795,794,795
  794 WRITE(6,738)((SDEV(L,KA),L=1.4),KA=20,38)
      GO TO 796
  795 WRITE(6,707)(SDEV(4,KA),KA=24,46
  796 CONTINUE
      WRITE(6,733)
      WRITE(6,740)
      IF(ITS)798,797,798
  797 WRITE(6,736)((SDEV(L,KA),L=1,4),KA=47,69)
      GO TO 799
  798 WRITE(6,707)(SDEV(4,KA),KA=47,69)
  799 CONTINUE
      WRITE(6,730)
      IF(ITS)1751,1750,1751
 1750 WRITE(6,754)
      GO TO 1754
 1751 IF(ITS-1)1753,1752,1753
 1752 WRITE(6,759)
      GO TO 1754
 1753 WRITE(6,758)
 1754 CONTINUE
  755 FORMAT(18X,24H *** COMBINED SAMPLE ***/)
  756 FORMAT(9H AVERAGES/)
  757 FORMAT(20H STANDARD DEVIATIONS/)
      WRITE(6,755)
      WRITE(6,906)
      WRITE(6,908)
      WRITE(6,910)
      WRITE(6,756)
      IF(ITS)765,997,765
  997 DO 764 J=1,23
  764 WRITE(6,739)(AV(I,J),I=1,3),NSIG(J+69),AV(4,J),U(J+69),VARAVT(J,1,
     14),VARAVT(J, 2,4),VARAVT(J,3,4)
      GO TO 766
  765 DO 1765 K=1,23
 1765 WRITE(6,737) AV(4,K),            VARAVT(K,1,4),VARAVT(K,2,4),VARAVT(K,
     13,4)
  766 CONTINUE
      WRITE(6,733)
      WRITE(6,757)
      IF(ITS)768,767,768
  676 WRITE(6,736)((TDEV(I,J),I=1,4),J=1,23)
      GO TO 769
  768 WRITE(6,707)(TDEV(4,J),J=1,23)
  769 CONTINUE
      IF(IRW)762,761,762
```

```
  762 IF(IRW-1)999,763,999
  761 IRW=1
      ITS=2
      GO TO 48
  763 IRW=1
      ITS=1
      GO TO 48
   20 WRITE(6,7) L
    7 FORMAT(15)
      GO TO 990
  999 CONTINUE
      END

  AC 1108 FORTRAN V COMPLICATION.    0 *DIAGNOSTIC* MESSAGE(S)
```

INDEX